Turkey

Editor Dale Gunthorp
Design Patrick Frean
Picture Research Maggie Colbeck
Production Philip Hughes
Illustrations Ron Hayward Associates
          John Shackell
          Marilyn Day
          John Mousdale
          Marshall Rumbaugh
Maps Matthews & Taylor Associates

Photographs Most of the pictures were provided by **Sonia Halliday** and **Laura Lushington,** who took photographs especially for this book.

Other photographic sources Key to position of illustrations: *(T)* top, *(C)* centre, *(B)* bottom, *(L)* left, *(R)* right. British Museum *41(BR)*; J. Allen Cash *9 (CR)*, *16(TR)*, *31(TL)*, *51(TR)*; Wm. Collins Sons and Co. *36(TR)*; Mary Evans Picture Library *40(BR)*, *42(BR)*, *50(T)*, *50(B)*; Peter Fraenkel *9(BR)*, *16(T)*; Ibbs and Tillett *36(TC)*; Keystone Press Agency *53(BR)*; Mansell Collection *44(TL)*, *56*; Radio Times Hulton Picture Library *44(BL)*; Turkish Embassy *44(BC)*, *45(TL)*, *52(T)*, *53(TL)*; World Health Organization *52(BL)*.

First published 1975
Macdonald Educational Limited,
Holywell House
London, E. C. 2

© Macdonald Educational
Limited 1975

ISBN 0-382-06116-0

Published in the United
States by Silver Burdett
Company, Morristown, N. J.
1977 Printing

Library of Congress
Catalog Card No. 77-70192

The **endpaper picture** shows Istanbul, looking across to the new Bosphorus Bridge, with the Asian shore in the distance.

Page 6 shows a typical Turkish market square. This square is in Usak (pronounced "Ushak"), in the western half of Anatolia.

Turkey

the land and its people

David Hotham

Macdonald Educational

Contents

Who are the Turks?

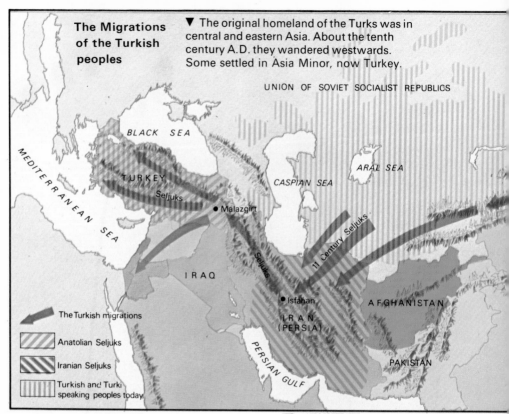

The Migrations of the Turkish peoples

▼ The original homeland of the Turks was in central and eastern Asia. About the tenth century A.D. they wandered westwards. Some settled in Asia Minor, now Turkey.

→ The Turkish migrations

▨ Anatolian Seljuks

▨ Iranian Seljuks

▥ Turkish and Turki speaking peoples today

The Turkish people

Basically the Turks are a Turanian people, whose original homeland was in central or eastern Asia. But the Turks of modern Turkey are so mixed with other more "western" peoples that they are really racially different from the "pure" Turks of Asia.

Towards the end of the eleventh century A.D. Turkish invaders from central Asia migrated westwards into Asia Minor, which at that time was part of the Byzantine (Eastern Roman) empire. They intermarried with the native peoples. These native peoples were a complicated mixture of all the races who had lived in Asia Minor before the Turkish invaders arrived. They included Hittites, Phrygians, Greeks, Celts, Armenians, Jews, Kurds, and others.

Before the Turks arrived Asia Minor was mainly Greek and Christian, but the Turks conquered the whole country, imposing on it their religion, Islam, and their language. The resultant mixture of peoples in Asia Minor is what we today call the "Turks". And Asia Minor became known as Turkey, after these Turkish settlers.

The Turks of Turkey

Any visitor travelling through Turkey, will notice that the Turks are racially very mixed: they are even more mixed than the English are, though not as much as the Americans. Some Turks are olive skinned with black hair and brown eyes. Others, of whom the most famous is the great reformer, Mustafa Kemal Atatürk himself, are blonde. Most Turks think of themselves as Europeans, rather than Asians. They may have a racial kinship with the Hungarians and the Finns, both of whom also came originally from the East.

But the Turks have looked westwards towards Europe ever since Atatürk westernized his country 50 years ago and made it part of Europe.

▲ A Kurdish peasant from the Lake Van area of Eastern Turkey. Several million Kurds live in this region, as well as in parts of Iraq and Persia. They are racially distinct from the Turks.

▶ The cloth market at Uşak, in western Anatolia, showing typical bright-coloured materials worn by Turkish peasant women. The men wear more austere clothes.

▲ Nomad (*Yürük*) women outside their goat-hair tent home, near Tarsus, in south Turkey. Nomads are tending to settle as the wandering life becomes more difficult. They have to rent winter pasture from the peasants, and, even in summer, good wild land is not always available in the mountains.

▶ Peasant women wearing baggy Shalvar trousers. Notice that the women are unveiled. Turkish peasant women are usually forthcoming. Veiled women are still occasionally seen in towns.

▼ Men at coffee-bar in Diyarbakir, south-east Turkey. Their faces are not Mongoloid (with slanting eyes), as are the faces of the Turkish races still in central Asia, for the Turkish settlers intermarried with earlier inhabitants of Anatolia.

A rugged and mountainous land

Anatolia and Thrace

Turkey is a large, mountainous and beautiful country. It is 780,570 square kilometres (301,380 square miles) in area, more than three times the size of Great Britain, and so rugged that only about a quarter is fit for cultivation.

The country is divided into two main parts, Anatolia (which used to be called Asia Minor), and Thrace. These two parts are separated from each other by the famous Straits of the Dardanelles and Bosphorus. This waterway is of great strategic importance, since it is the only passage Russian ships can use to pass from the Black Sea into the Mediterranean. On the Straits stands the famous city of Istanbul, formerly called Constantinople, which has belonged to Turkey since the year 1453.

The particular beauty of the countryside in Turkey is due to the diversity of the climate in different parts. The Black Sea coast in the north has wonderful forests and vegetation like France; western and southern Turkey are warm like the Mediterranean; the central plateau is a dry steppe like parts of Asia; south eastern Turkey has hot semi-deserts; eastern Turkey has high mountains.

In eastern Turkey the mountains culminate in the peak of Mount Ararat (5,151 metres), the mountain on which, according to the Bible, the Ark of Noah rested after the Flood.

Classical sites

Turkey is very rich in sites of classical antiquity, many of them associated with the early days of Christianity. For example, places like Ephesus, Antioch, Caesarea and Iconium, as well as Troy, Miletus, Sardis and the Cilician Gates, are all in Turkey. Many of these places are associated with historic figures such as St. Paul or Alexander the Great. Turkey is also a wonderful place for wild flowers, birds and animals. Some of it is more or less unexplored, or is still roamed by nomads.

The variety of Turkey

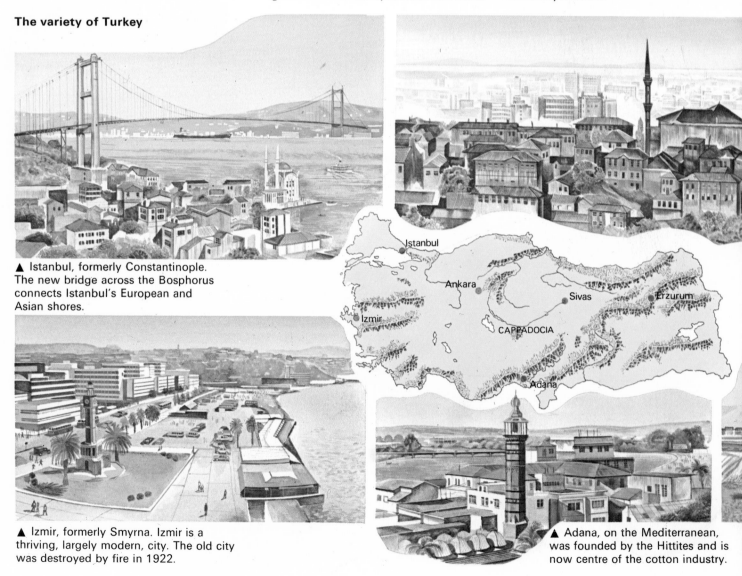

▲ Istanbul, formerly Constantinople. The new bridge across the Bosphorus connects Istanbul's European and Asian shores.

▲ Izmir, formerly Smyrna. Izmir is a thriving, largely modern, city. The old city was destroyed by fire in 1922.

▲ Adana, on the Mediterranean, was founded by the Hittites and is now centre of the cotton industry.

◀ Ankara, capital of Turkey, was a slow-moving provincial town before Atatürk made it capital of Turkey in 1923.

▲ Tobacco nursery at Nazilli in the Aegean region of western Turkey. More women than men work in agriculture. The Aegean is one of the main tobacco-growing areas.

▼ A bay and dwellings at Alanya, on the south coast of Turkey. This coastline, backed by the Taurus mountains, receives most of its rain in winter.

▲ Mountain road in eastern Turkey. In this part of Turkey villages are often snowed up for several months in winter. Wolves and bears live in the mountains.

▲ Erzurum has a rigorous mountain climate. It has Seljuk and Ottoman buildings, made from the hard local grey stone.

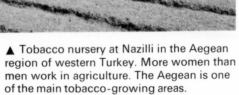

▲ Cappadocia has a weird, wind eroded landscape. People still live in homes carved in caves of living rock.

Family life

Respect for parents

Family life is still extremely important in Turkey, and solidarity between members of a family is very strong. Turkish family life is based on respect for parents and grand-parents. This respect applies at all ages. For example, a man of fifty will not smoke a cigarette or sit with his legs crossed in the presence of his own father. As several generations usually live in the same house, parents have great power in the home.

The importance of sons

Until quite recently, the only task of a peasant wife which was considered really important was to have a son. Girls were regarded by their parents as a disaster. Turkish peasant fathers when asked how many children they had, would often not even mention the daughters.

The strongest personal relationship in a Turkish family is between the mother and the son, but for an adult man the most important bond is with his brothers or other nearest male relations. There are often financial links within this extended family.

Except in westernized circles, Turkish marriages are still usually arranged between the parents. But in parts of Turkey, instead of the bride bringing a dowry, as once in Europe, the bridegroom's family often pays a large sum of money for the bride. This ancient custom, is known as "bride price". Peasant women work in the fields, and peasants consider that the price paid for a girl is a reasonable return for the work she will do.

But there are many very advanced women in modern Turkey, such as women judges, members of parliament, artists, journalists and others. Women were given equality in the law by Atatürk 50 years ago. Old customs still restrict women, but they have more opportunity to use their rights.

The peasant family's day

5 a.m.

The peasant family rises early during the growing season, for there is much to do in the fields. After breakfast, the children walk to the village school, while both parents attend to their plots. Lunch is often eaten in the fields. In the after-noon the children might help on the farm, till the setting sun sent them home. Father might then go to the local coffee house, while mother prepares the meal. Everyone would be in bed not long after 9p.m.

12 noon

5 p.m.

9 p.m.

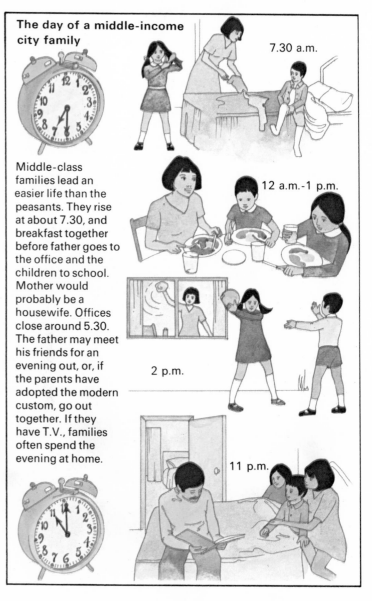

The day of a middle-income city family

7.30 a.m.

Middle-class families lead an easier life than the peasants. They rise at about 7.30, and breakfast together before father goes to the office and the children to school. Mother would probably be a housewife. Offices close around 5.30. The father may meet his friends for an evening out, or, if the parents have adopted the modern custom, go out together. If they have T.V., families often spend the evening at home.

12 a.m.-1 p.m.

2 p.m.

11 p.m.

▲ Ploughing time for a Turkish peasant family. Women do much of the work in the fields, and children are often taken away from school to help.

◄ A group of boys in the town of Kaş in south-west Turkey playing in the street after school.

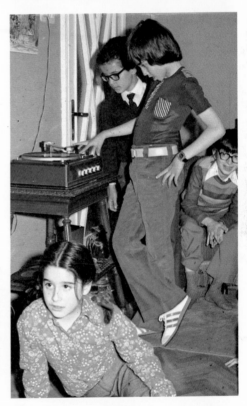

▲ In the cities, wealthier families live much as people do in the richer countries of the West. These are the children of a successful businessman in Istanbul. Their possessions include such luxury items as record players and games like Monopoly. However, unlike a comparable American or British family, they have domestic servants.

◄ A peasant family inside its home at Labraunda. Turkish family ties are very close, and fathers take great interest in their children.

Leisure in town and village

The talent for enjoying life

The Turks are a serious and dignified-looking people, but they also have a great talent for enjoying themselves and for human relationships. They are somewhat like the Lowland Scots in the contrast between their usual rather restrained behaviour and "when they let their hair down".

Turks enjoy most of the same things as people do in the West, such as watching football matches, going to the cinema or theatre, reading newspapers, or looking at television. At the moment T.V. covers only the three biggest cities, Ankara, Istanbul and Izmir, but many more stations are being built which will soon reach the whole country. As many Turkish households do not yet have T.V., one often sees sets in the streets of the cities surrounded by crowds watching perhaps football or a wrestling match.

Strolling and coffee drinking

Turks particularly love strolling or sauntering in large groups along streets or boulevards, not because they are going anywhere in particular, but simply because they like it. They are also very fond of paying visits, and giving presents. Turks usually do not thank for presents, the reason for this being to show that the pleasure of the visit comes from seeing the friend, not from the gift he brings.

Drinking Turkish coffee is of course a universal pleasure, almost a ritual. Turkish men love sitting around in coffee houses, playing cards or backgammon, or listening to sad Turkish music blaring from a radio set. City dwellers enjoy night-life, and belly-dancing is very popular. Turks also love dancing; some of their native dances are fascinating and very wild.

▲ Sitting in the coffee bar, sipping strong Turkish coffee, and passionately debating every imaginable subject, is the most popular leisure activity for Turkish men. Women are very seldom seen there.

▼ Belly-dancing is still a popular side of Turkish night-life. The trained belly-dancer can make the most amazing contortions with her body.

Some Turkish pastimes

▲ Turks love to while away an evening in a comfortable restaurant, talking, or listening to Turkish music.

▲ Water sellers in Istanbul. Life in the streets is very varied. Water sellers, and other street vendors do a brisk trade.

▲ Relaxing in a Turkish bath. Turkish baths or *hammams*, are not so frequently used as they were in the past. *Hammams* are hot steam baths for taking off superfluous fat; they make one feel very healthy and clean.

▲ Swimmers at the Bosphorus. Turks are keen swimmers, and their country has fine sandy beaches. The Bosphorus is traversed by strong currents, and is not the best place for a swim.

▼ Shoe shiners are a common sight in the streets. Many of them have splendid brass boxes for their brushes and polish. For very little money they make a first class job of one's shoes.

▲ Strolling in the streets, without any special aim or destination, is a popular Turkish pastime.

Bazaars and markets

The bakkal

Supermarkets and multiple stores are only a recent development in Turkey, and many shoppers make all their basic purchases from a small shop, selling simple commodities. They know the shop-keeper, and the shop-keeper knows his customer's needs.

For the average Turkish housewife the most important shop is the *bakkal*, or grocer, which stocks a wide assortment of goods. He sells everything needed for daily fare: bread, nuts, cheese, fruit, coffee, tea, vegetables, rice, olive oil, tinned foods and sausages. Raki, beer, vodka, cheap wine and cigarettes would also be on his shelves.

Turks used to eat little meat, fish or eggs, but lived mostly on bread, fruit, vegetables, and milk products. Today people eat more animal protein. There are many different fruits and vegetables in Turkey thanks to the diversity of the climate. These include oranges, lemons, bananas, apples, pears, pomegranates, grapes, olives, figs, green peppers, red peppers, cucumbers and watermelons. Turkish greengrocers are most artistic in the way they lay out their stalls.

Turkish bread is particularly good, and the Turks eat a vast amount of it. Yet, surprisingly, they are not often overweight.

Bazaars and carpets

In Istanbul the most famous of all shopping places is the Great Covered Bazaar, or *Buyuk Kapali Charshi* as it is known in Turkish. This consists of hundreds of small shops selling jewellery, leatherware, gold and silver ornaments, carpets, copper pots, meerschaum, and alabaster objects, and almost everything you can think of for the home. It is a great tourist attraction.

All over Turkey there are shops specialising in carpets, and in the hand-woven rugs known as *kilims*. Turkish quilts are also famous. Home-produced Turkish textiles, and of course towels, are excellent. Turkish shoes are good, and there are many first class cheap tailors. *Mohair* is a speciality, and is clipped off special goats with shiny fleeces which live in the region around Ankara.

Turkish money

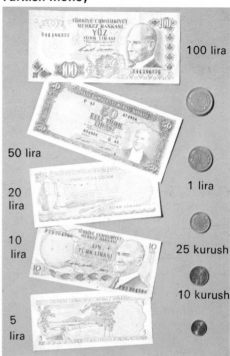

100 lira

50 lira

20 lira

10 lira

5 lira

1 lira

25 kurush

10 kurush

▲ Turkish money is divided into liras and kurush. One lira is divided into 100 kurush. The Turkish lira is worth about three English pence.

▼ Fish market near the Galata bridge in Istanbul. The sea around Istanbul is rich in edible fish, including mackerel, turbot, bonito, tuna and anchovy.

The living standards of Turkish families

▲ The brush market in Istanbul. These brushes are used everywhere for housework in Turkey. They are hand made, and are most effective sweepers.

▼ Fruit stall in Bursa. There is an extraordinary variety of fruit in Turkey. Peaches predominate in the Bursa region, where they are the main fruit product.

▲ A quilt shop in the covered bazaar in Bursa, north-west Turkey. These quilts are very popular. The colourful display in the shop is typical.

▲ For urban families, major expenses are food, rent and transport.

▲ Peasants often own their small homes, and pay no rent. They spend little money because their farms provide 60% of their needs, and they may barter produce with other peasants for some of the extras.

The great Turkish cuisine

Enjoying good food

The Turks claim that their cooking is one of the three main cuisines of the world—along with the French and the Chinese. Turks enjoy good food, and their cooking takes many original forms.

Probably the best-known single Turkish dish is *shish kebab*, which is made out of cubes of lamb roasted on a skewer over a charcoal fire (the original barbecue). Another one is *yoghurt*.

Turks in the city like to have breakfast at about 8 a.m., usually olives and white cheese, often with a glass of home-grown Turkish tea. The midday meal, at noon, will often consist of *dolmas*, meat or rice wrapped in vine-leaves or cabbage-leaves, or possibly *beurreks*, which are fine sheets of slightly salted pastry mixed with cheese, meat, or spinach, and flavoured with herbs.

Aubergine, called *patlican* in Turkey, is a special favourite, and there are said to be over a hundred different ways of cooking it. Many of these have picturesque names, such as *Sultan beyendi* meaning "What the Sultan liked", or *Imam bayildi*, "the Imam swooned"—presumably from delight at so delicious a dish!

Mezeh and raki

In Turkey there are small restaurants all over the country where the customer is normally taken into the kitchen and shown the various foods sizzling in their pans, so that he can choose what he wants. There are also many first-class restaurants which cook western food.

One of the best dishes is the Turkish hors d'oeuvre, known as *mezeh*. They are particularly good with wine or raki, and Turks love to sit in the evening, chatting over their *mezeh* and wine, enjoying just being alive.

Make yourself a Turkish meal

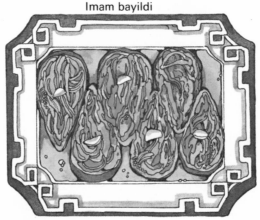
Imam bayildi

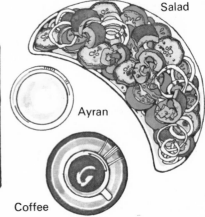
Salad

Ayran

Coffee

CACIK (pronounced "jajik")

Cold yoghurt and cucumber
(to serve 4)

1 medium sized cucumber
¾ pint yoghurt (2 tubs)
1½ teaspoons vinegar
½ teaspoon chopped dill
1½ teaspoons finely chopped mint
1 teaspoon olive oil
Salt

This should be prepared at least two hours before the time of the meal. Wash and peel the cucumber, then slice it lengthways and scoop out the seeds with a teaspoon. Grate the cucumber on the coarsest side of a cheese grater. Pour the yoghurt into a deep bowl, and stir it briskly until it is smooth and creamy in texture. Mix the oil, salt, dill, vinegar and cucumber in with the yoghurt, stirring gently. Taste the mixture and add a little more salt if necessary. Put the mixture into the refrigerator, and allow it to chill for at least two hours. Chill the bowls (use soup bowls) before serving, add an ice cube to each portion, and garnish with the mint. Serve before the main meal, as a cold soup.

IMAM BAYILDI
Braised aubergines with tomatoes and onions
2 medium sized aubergines (as long and narrow as possible)
4 medium sized onions
4 tomatoes
4 tablespoons olive oil
2 cloves of garlic, chopped
Parsley, chopped ; salt

Cut off the stalks of the aubergines, and slice them lengthways. Make four slits in the fleshy part of each half. Slice the onions into rings. (Wet them under the cold tap if they make your eyes water.) Peel the tomatoes. Then chop the tomatoes, and mix with the onions, salt and garlic. Force as much as possible of the mixture into the slits in the aubergine halves, and arrange the rest on top. Pour the oil and a small cup of water into a large flat casserole or pan. Place the aubergines into the pan carefully. Bring to the boil, then turn the heat low, and put the lid on the pan. Simmer for at least an hour. The dish may be eaten hot, though the Turks serve it at room temperature. It should be sprinkled with parsley.

RICE PILAV
1 cup long grain rice
2 oz butter
2 cups stock (chicken or vegetable)
½ teaspoon salt
Sprinkling of black pepper

Melt half the butter in a pan, then add the raw rice and stir until all the grains are coated in melted butter. Add the stock, salt, pepper and half a cup of water. Bring to the boil, then simmer till all the water has been absorbed. This should take about 20 minutes. Stir in the rest of the butter, and toss lightly with a fork. Serve hot or cold.

SALAD
This can be made with whatever suitable vegetables are in season. The principal ingredients of Turkish salads are tomatoes, cucumber, green peppers and lettuce. The dressing should be made of lemon juice and a little oil.

AYRAN
This delicious drink is made of yoghurt, diluted with water till it has the consistency of buttermilk, and mixed with a little salt. It is an excellent accompaniment to the meal.

► Turkish chef in the kitchen of a small restaurant. It is the custom in Turkey to take customers into the kitchen and show them the various foods available.

Typical meals for a weekday

Breakfast: white cheese and olives, with bread and tea or coffee.

Lunch: vine leaves or cabbage leaves stuffed with mince meat and rice.

Supper: soup, shish kebab. Döner kebab. Perhaps chicken with rice. Some sweet dish such as baklava or tel kadayif.

▲ One of the most popular dishes in Turkey is döner kebab: lamb's meat turned on a spit (*doner* means turning) in front of hot coals. It is cut off in flakes with a sharp knife.

Some famous Turkish dishes

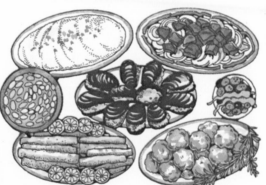

▲ **Mezeh** are Turkish hors d'oeuvre. They come in various forms, including mussels, anchovies, Circassian chicken (chicken with walnuts), meat balls, paprikas and fish.

▲ **Kebab:** there are many varieties of kebab. Shish kebab consists of chunks of lamb on a skewer with green pepper, cucumber and tomato, often highly spiced.

▲ A **crayfish** dish. Shellfish of many different kinds are a speciality in Istanbul and the coastal regions of Turkey. Very little fish is eaten by the peasants.

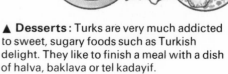

▲ **Desserts:** Turks are very much addicted to sweet, sugary foods such as Turkish delight. They like to finish a meal with a dish of halva, baklava or tel kadayif.

Education gateway to advancement

The spread of education

There is a great popular demand for education in Turkey, where it is regarded as the chief means to social advancement. Turks call it the gateway to civilization.

Illiteracy is still high, and 52 per cent of the population can neither read nor write. There is a great shortage of teachers, and the birthrate is high, so some children still receive little or no schooling even though school attendance is compulsory in law. Furthermore, in the remoter parts of the country, some peasants take their children away from school before they have completed their compulsory five year period. The parents believe their children will be more useful helping out at home, and it is difficult for the Government to persuade them otherwise. However, development in education is pressing ahead, and soon all young people should receive primary schooling.

Children start school at the age of six. In 1973, there were 5,300,000 pupils in primary schools. In addition to basic knowledge, Turkish primary schools teach simple agricultural and technical information. Due to the shortage of teachers there is often serious over-crowding, with more than 100 pupils per class.

Secondary and higher education

Secondary education lasts for six years after the age of 11. Three of these are spent in a middle school and another three in a *lycée*. In 1973 a million children attended middle schools and 300,000 attended *lycées*. There are now ten universities in Turkey, and also provision for higher vocational and technical education.

One of the most controversial of all subjects in Turkey is religious education. The great reformer Kemal Atatürk abolished it altogether, as part of his plan to reduce the influence of Islam. But it has crept back, and is now the subject of furious debate.

▲ Turkish children coming out of school. Boys of this age are not at all shy and will engage foreigners in conversation.

▼ Mixed class of boys and girls in a Turkish middle school in Ankara. Owing to the shortage of teachers, classes are often large.

The Turkish school system

Primary schools are the most important part of the Turkish school system, and every child is required by law to spend five years at primary school. After that, pupils may spend three years at a middle school, before attending a *lycée*, and then going on to college or university.

University

Vocational and technical

Lycée 14-16 years

Middle school 11-13 years

There are far more pupils in primary schools (over five million in 1973) than in higher sectors. Middle schools and *lycées* had 300,000 pupils in 1973. Village schools teach farming as well as academic subjects.

Village schools

Town schools

Primary school 6-10 years

5,300,000 pupils in 1973

▲ A party of Turkish students being shown the ruins of Ephesus. Considerable effort is made to teach young people about pre-Turkish civilizations of Anatolia. The proportion of women students has greatly increased.

► The faculties of History and Languages at the University of Ankara. The statue in the foreground is that of the great Ottoman architect Sinan. Traditionally statues were forbidden by Islam, though statues of Atatürk are often found.

The Muslim tradition

The religion of Islam

The Turks are Muslims, followers of the religion of Islam (Mohammedanism). Islam was founded by the prophet Mohammed. God is called Allah; the Koran is the holy book and people worship in a mosque.

Mosques in Turkey, like many churches in Europe, are often very old and beautiful buildings, and are made still more beautiful by the minarets which are attached to them. These are very tall slender towers, looking rather like gigantic pencils standing on end. From the top of these minarets an official called the *muezzin* calls people to prayer, not once a week, but five times a *day*. The sound of the muezzin's voice calling people to prayer is one of the most familiar sounds in Turkey. It sounds very different from the ringing of church bells, and is perhaps more beautiful.

Fasts and sacrifices

Turks are naturally religious. Most of them keep the fast in the month of Ramadan, during which they may not eat or drink, or even smoke a cigarette, between sunrise and sunset. Most Turkish families also kill an animal, usually a sheep, for the yearly *Kurban Bayram*, the Feast of the Sacrifice, which is the most holy religious festival of the year.

There are no priests in Islam, but there are prayer-leaders known as Imams, who conduct services in the mosques and preach sermons. These Imams often have great influence among the peasants, who are very devout.

One result of Turkey being a Muslim country is that, although there are many kinds of animals—sheep, cows and horses—pigs are seldom seen. Pigs are regarded by Muslims as unclean, and to eat their flesh is forbidden.

Kemal Atatürk, the great Turkish reformer made Turkey into a secular state. Islam, no longer the official religion, became only a matter for the private person. He abolished polygamy and closed down the Dervish sects, which had been a feature of Ottoman religious fervour.

▲ The Suleymaniye mosque in Istanbul. This is one of the largest and finest of all the Ottoman mosques, built by the famous architect Sinan in the sixteenth century. It is usually illuminated for holidays.

▶ The vast majority of Turks are Muslims though it should be remembered that about 7 million of the population are followers of the Alevi (Shi'a) sect as distinct from the orthodox Sunni Muslims.

▼ Muslims washing before prayer at a fountain outside the Green Mosque in Bursa. Cleanliness before prayer is of extreme importance in Islam, a religion in which external rituals play a great part.

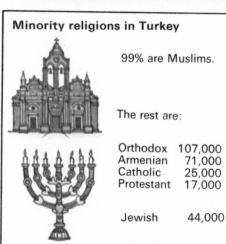

Minority religions in Turkey

99% are Muslims.

The rest are:

Orthodox	107,000
Armenian	71,000
Catholic	25,000
Protestant	17,000
Jewish	44,000

▲ Muezzin calling the faithful to prayer from the top of the minaret. Many minarets have amplifiers to relay the call.

▼ An Imam leading the congregation inside the mosque. Islam has no priests: the Imam is a prayer leader.

▲ Turk praying in a mosque in south Turkey. Muslims do not have to pray in mosques, and often do so in the open.

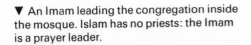

▲ The Dervishes always whirl in an anti-clockwise direction. Long practice is needed to become an adept. The dance is intended to achieve mystical union with God.

Customs and superstitions

Beware the evil eye

Many superstitions still practised among the peasantry have descended from ancient religious beliefs. Magical rituals for bringing rain, for instance, are common among peasants living on the dry steppes of Anatolia. Ancient customs connected with marriage and childbirth survive in many parts of the country; and even in large towns old recipes to frighten away illness are sometimes followed.

The most powerful of all superstitions, and the one connected with most ritual practices is the evil eye. Turks call it *Nazar*, or the "look". It is thought that people can "put the evil eye" on one, even without meaning any harm. So the safest thing seems to be to keep out of the limelight, and wear protective charms, called *muskas*.

Blue beads are worn by children and animals to keep the evil eye at bay. Blue beads and tortoise shells are often hung beside the driver's seat in buses and taxis. Babies are thought to be in special danger. If a child is praised, the evil eye might take an interest. So people say "*Maashallah*", meaning "God has worked wonders", just to remind the evil eye that the child is under God's protection. Sometimes, for luck, a tortoise may be put under the baby's pillow. In remote areas, some peasant mothers make their babies look as ugly and dirty as possible, to make them less interesting to the evil eye.

Turbans and veils

Dress has been a controversial matter in Turkey, particularly since Atatürk banned the fez and discouraged the veil. Atatürk wanted to reduce the influence of Islam, which he thought was preventing Turkey from developing. Today older customs of dress have crept back in some of the towns, and it is no longer unusual to see women go about with their faces veiled by a *charshaf*. This is a headscarf drawn partly across the face. So in Turkey one sees many different customs of dress, from the baggy trousers of the peasant women, to city suits, and even veils.

▲ Young children are thought to be especially in danger from the Evil Eye. Visitors to Turkey should remember never to praise a child in front of its parents without saying the protective word "Maashallah" (God has worked wonders). Children and domestic animals sometimes wear blue beads to ward off the evil eye.

◄ Peasants who migrate to the cities usually run up rough shacks to live in. Once they have got the roof on, their houses are safe from demolition by the authorities.

▼ Tame bears are often to be seen in Turkey, led by gypsies or tinkers. They perform dances to the music of tambourines, or pretend to wrestle with their keepers. Bears are very popular animals in Turkey and many stories are told about them.

▲ Newborn babies are sometimes rubbed over with salt to make them strong. In the first 40 days of its life an infant must be able to resist the evil eye and other malign influences.

▼ In the villages it has been known for young men to seize girls and run away with them. This is often because they cannot afford the "bride price". There may be legal consequences, or a vendetta.

◄ An old man smoking the "hubble-bubble" water pipe in a coffee house. The smoke is cooled by being drawn through water. The water pipe is rarely seen today, and is mainly smoked by old men who enjoy the customs and rituals of more leisurely days.

▲ Turkish dances are often extremely wild and fantastic, and this sword dance from the Bursa region of north-west Turkey is typical. Many dances have their origins in the pre-Islamic folk lore of the central Asian Turks.

Heroes of a proud past

Deeds of bravery

Many old Turkish myths and legends go back centuries to times long before the Turks arrived in Anatolia, when they lived in central Asia, or near China. The oldest of these legends is that of Dedeh Korkut, a hero who performed wonderful deeds of bravery against impossible odds. These stories may be modelled on a real person who lived in those nomadic times.

Memed, the outlaw

A completely modern Turkish hero is "Slim Memed", chief figure of a celebrated story by the writer Yashar Kemal. Memed became leader of a band of brigands and saved the oppressed peasants from wicked feudal landowners. This story has a strong social message, and vehemently attacks the system of land distribution which left the peasants with the worst and most barren land.

Other modern heroes are Zeki Muren, a famous singer, and Yilmaz Güney, a left-wing filmstar who has been in prison for his political views.

But perhaps the most famous of all Turkish popular figures is Nasreddin Hodja, a legendary sage and jester, whose jokes or philosophical remarks are known by all Turks and constantly quoted everywhere.

▲ The myths of Dedeh Korkut are a collection of old Turkish legends which tell of the heroic deeds of the Turks in the days when they lived in the mountains and deserts of central Asia. Dedeh Korkut and his men performed wonderful deeds against the enemies of the Turks, driving them out of their territory. Every schoolboy knows these tales which are so closely associated with the pride of the Turks in their race.

▶ The adventures of Nasreddin Hodja, a fourteenth century sage and jester, are among Turkey's most famous legends. Hodja has a philosophical, though not always moral, cast of mind, and usually wins over opponents because of his ready wit. The tale of Hodja and the cooking pot is typical: One day Hodja borrowed a pot from his neighbour. When he returned it, the neighbour found a second, smaller pot inside. "Your pot has had a baby," Hodja said casually. The next time Hodja needed a pot, the neighbour was more than ready to lend it to him, but when the time came to return it Hodja was empty handed. "I'm afraid your pot died," he said. The neighbour complained that this was absurd, but Hodja came back with unanswerable logic, telling the neighbour that he had believed a pot could give birth, and one who accepts the fact of birth must also accept death.

◀ The legend of Koroglu is one of the most famous of all in Turkey. Koroglu was an outlaw rather like Robin Hood, who helped the common people in their struggle against officialdom. His main enemy was the Bey of Bolu, a local potentate rather like the Sheriff of Nottingham in the Robin Hood story.

▼ A scene from the shooting of the film *Dubious Patriots*, with the Turkish film stars Fikret Hakan (here being filmed), and Salih Güney, as well as American stars including Tony Curtis. Heroes of the screen are much admired in Turkey.

▲ A characteristic painting of Atatürk in full evening dress, hanging from buildings on a national holiday. Statues and paintings honouring Turkey's greatest modern hero are found all over Turkey.

▶ A postage stamp showing *Karagöz*, the shadow puppet. The shadow theatre was introduced to Turkey in Ottoman times. Puppet shows were very popular in Turkey, before the days of cinema and T.V.

POSTA

1967 TURİZM YILI

100 KURUŞ

TÜRKİYE CUMHURİYETİ

AJANS-TÜRK MATBAASI / ANKARA

Getting about in Turkey

▼ There are domestic air services from Ankara or Istanbul to all the main Turkish cities, and outside Turkey there are international flights to major European cities including London and Paris. Turkey has a fleet of Boeing jets, as well as smaller craft, used largely on domestic flights, and including Fokkers and DC planes.

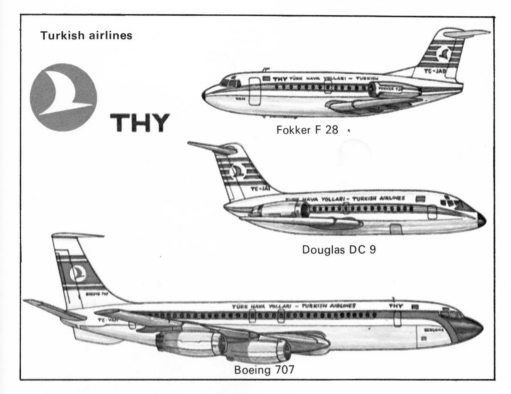

Turkish airlines

THY

Fokker F 28

Douglas DC 9

Boeing 707

Donkeys to Boeings

Turkish methods of transport are very varied, ranging from donkeys and ox-carts with solid wheels in the villages, to DC 10s and Boeing 707s on Turkish Airlines. The internal airways extend to all the 15 main Turkish cities, and a network of good roads also covers most of the country.

Turkey has more than 60,000 kilometres of all-weather highways and 170,000 km of secondary roads. Motoring is a pleasure because the roads are wide and fairly free of traffic, and drivers are very helpful to motorists in trouble.

Engineering achievements

In a country so mountainous as Turkey, some of the roads are amazing engineering achievements. One example of this is the dizzy corniche which runs right along the south Turkish coast, and another is the spectacularly beautiful Zigana pass which leads from the rugged old fortress of Erzurum, in eastern Turkey, up to the Black Sea coast. Turkish bus services are cheap and efficient, with excellent imperturbable drivers. Strong nerves are needed on some of the mountain routes. Most buses and lorries have the words "Trust in Allah" or "Maashallah" written on the front of them to bring luck.

A feature of transport in the cities are the *dolmus* taxis (pronounced "dolmush" meaning "full"), which fill up with people before they move off, then pick up and drop off passengers all along the route.

▲ The main Ankara-Istanbul road near the Ankara end. This is typical Anatolian country, with bare hillsides and poplar trees in the valleys. The main roads of Turkey are well-surfaced.

▶ A pair of buffaloes pulling a log cart by Lake Abant in northern Turkey. Buffaloes are much used by the peasantry for the heaviest loads, and they are considered stronger than oxen.

▲ Diesel trains approaching Istanbul, and large and small shipping in the Bosphorus. Turkish railways have some fast diesel trains (called *motorlü tren*), but travel across country is slow because the railway winds to avoid the many mountains and deep valleys and diverts to stop at country towns. There are first, second and third class compartments for passengers. Some mountainous areas on the coast have no rail connections, and rely on coastal shipping as their main means of communication. Boats service the Black Sea and Mediterranean coasts.

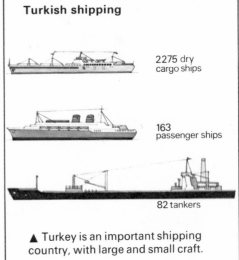

Turkish shipping

2275 dry cargo ships

163 passenger ships

82 tankers

▲ Turkey is an important shipping country, with large and small craft.

◄ A well loaded *dolmuş* (full) taxi about to depart. *Dolmuş* taxis are marked with a yellow stripe. During the rush hour, people throng the *dolmuş* ranks, while drivers call out the routes they plan to take, and how many more customers they can accommodate.

Sports of a martial people

The football fanatics

Being a martial and virile people, the Turks are particularly fond of sport. The most popular sport in Turkey as in many other countries, is football. League matches in Turkey usually arouse intense emotions, and sometimes degenerate into wild riots. Football pools, known in Turkey by the name of "Spor-Toto", are the most popular form of gambling.

Apart from football, other highly popular sports are volleyball, basketball, skiing, riding, swimming, tennis and cycling. Motor-racing and horse-racing are also important spectator sports. The importance of all these activities was recognized in 1970 by the creation of Turkey's first Ministry of Sport. There are now nearly 2,000 sporting clubs in Turkey.

One particular Turkish sport is the very ancient native game called *cirit* (pronounced "jirit"), a sort of jousting in which riders catch javelins thrown at them as they pass each other at full gallop. It is very dramatic to watch, but is now gradually dying out.

Champion wrestlers

One very typical and important sport in Turkey is wrestling, for which the Turks are particularly gifted, and have won many Olympic medals in recent years. The special Turkish form of this sport is known as "greased wrestling", in which the contestants wear long tight leather breeches and pour olive oil over themselves to make the holds more difficult.

Every year in the month of June the greased wrestling championships are held on an island near the city of Adrianople, in Thrace, in order to determine the chief wrestler of the year. The contests are accompanied by the music of pipes and drums and attract large crowds.

Hunting and shooting

Hunting and shooting are also very popular in Turkey, both for big and small game. Big game includes bear, wild boar, wild cat, deer and gazelle. There are said to be still a few panther and even leopard in the mountains.

Turkey's most popular international sports

Football

Volleyball

Basketball

Skiing

Riding

Swimming

Tennis

Cycling

Motor-racing

Horse-racing

▶ An international match, between the Turkish town of Izmir, and the Italian team from Bologna. Here the Izmir goalkeeper saves a drive from the Bologna forward.

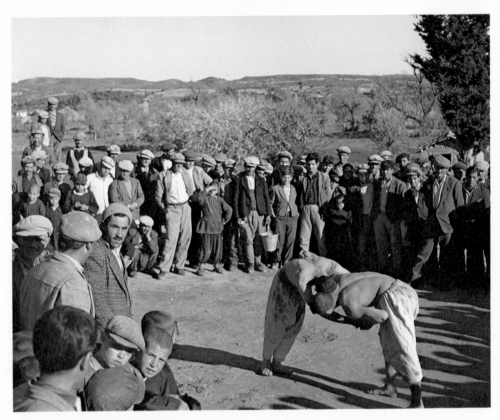

▲ The main ski resort is Mount Olympus (Uludag) in north-west Anatolia. Skiing is increasing rapidly in popularity in Turkey, both for Turks and tourists. Turkey has many snowy mountains.

▲ A wrestling match in a Turkish village during the dry summer. Wrestling is a very popular sport in Turkey and the Turks are very gifted at it.

▼ Boar hunting in the mountains of western Turkey. Peasants never eat boar, although it is very good, because of the Muslim taboo on pig meat.

▶ Cirit, the swift-moving winter game on ponies, requires excellent horsemanship and a good eye. The players throw wooden javelins at their opponents, and each hit is worth one point.

New industry and old crafts

Products of the craftsmen

Carpets, as one might expect, are still one of Turkey's main products. The Turks are very "carpet-minded". A young woman is usually given a carpet when she marries and simple households could almost be said to be "built round the carpet".

Carpet-making is a very old art which came originally from central Asia, and was brought by the Seljuk Turks into Anatolia. Most Turkish carpets are hand-made, the skills being passed on from one generation to another. Small girls start weaving at the age of seven. "Little hands tie tighter knots" it is said.

Leather products are one of Turkey's oldest handicrafts. There are excellent cheap leather coats and other leather goods in Turkey, made from the hides of sheep and goats.

One interesting Turkish product is made from the white clay deposit known as meerschaum, which is mined in the Eskisehir region of western Anatolia. Turkey is the only country where meerschaum is found in commercial quantities. It is made into pipes.

Industry and farming

Mining is one of the most important industries, especially iron and chrome ore. Turkey is the world's largest single producer of chrome ore. Today Turkey also produces machinery, chemicals, and other products of modern industry.

Tobacco and cotton are widely-grown crops. Turkey is the second largest exporter of tobacco in the world (after the U.S.A.). Turkish tobacco is highly valued because of its low nicotine content. There are many other agricultural products, such as sultanas, figs, grapes, hazelnuts and pistachio nuts.

One crop which has a dubious reputation is the opium poppy, grown in western Anatolia. Some of it is processed into medicine. The Turks themselves do not smoke opium, but part of the crop is illegally exported and made into heroin and morphine abroad.

▲ Container van of a Turkish fruit-exporting company loading grapes for export to Germany.

▼ Peasant women in colourful costumes harvesting in the Black Sea area. Turkish women work as much as men in the fields.

Turkey's mineral wealth

▼ After agriculture, Turkey's greatest wealth is in minerals, some of which are relatively unexploited.

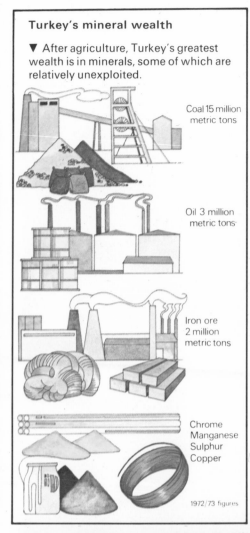

Coal 15 million metric tons

Oil 3 million metric tons·

Iron ore 2 million metric tons

Chrome
Manganese
Sulphur
Copper

1972/73 figures

▲ The "Anadol", Turkey's first passenger motor car. The 5-seater car was designed by a British firm, and is made of fibreglass, which makes it half the weight of a normal metal car.

▼ Wine press in Izmir. Wine has been produced in Anatolia for about 6,000 years. Turkey is now fifth world producer of wine, exporting 6 million litres a year.

▲ Women sorting tobacco leaves in a factory in Izmir. Turkey is the world's second largest exporter of tobacco (after the U.S.A.). Turkish tobacco is valued because it has a very low nicotine content, and the cigarettes have an excellent flavour.

Istanbul
city of empires

Skyline of domes and minarets

Many people think Istanbul is the most beautiful and extraordinary city on earth, because of its unique situation on the sea, its long history, and its world-famous skyline of domes and minarets.

The Roman Emperor Constantine made it the eastern capital of the Roman Empire in 324 A.D., on the site of Byzantium. For about 800 years it was the capital of the Byzantine empire. The Turks, who captured it from the Byzantines in 1453 A.D., made it their capital until 1923.

Istanbul is not quite a typical Turkish city, because the real Turkish homeland is in Anatolia. But it is Turkey's biggest city (pop. 3 million), and the heart of Turkish commerce and industry, as well as being the country's main tourist attraction.

The most famous building in Istanbul is Santa Sophia, the "Church of the Holy Wisdom", which was built in the sixth century A.D. by another Roman emperor Justinian. When the Turks captured Istanbul in 1453 they turned Santa Sophia into a mosque, by adding four minarets. Today it is a museum, and flooded with sightseers, but it is still considered a very holy place by both Christians and Muslims.

Five hundred mosques

Two other famous buildings are the Blue Mosque and the Suleymaniye Mosque, both constructed by Ottoman sultans. Apart from these there are about 500 other mosques, and countless other monuments from the Roman, Byzantine, and Ottoman civilizations.

Modern Istanbul is an amazing muddle of swirling traffic, jostling crowds, hooting steamers, and perspiring tourists. Travellers arriving by ship or train will have their luggage seized by immensely strong Turkish porters, called *hammals*, who carry everything on their backs. A Turkish *hammal* has even been seen carrying a grand piano!

Some places of special interest in Istanbul

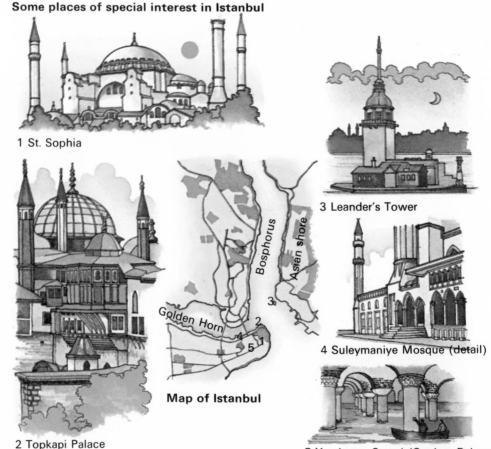

1 St. Sophia

2 Topkapi Palace

3 Leander's Tower

4 Suleymaniye Mosque (detail)

5 Yerebatan Sarayi (Sunken Palace)

Map of Istanbul

34

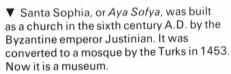

▲ The Galata Bridge, with the mosques of Stamboul behind. The Galata and Atatürk bridges cross the Golden Horn. Though the bridge seems busy, at rush hours it is ten times as crowded. Both ends are thronged with pedlars.

▲ View from the Suleymaniye mosque showing Galata Bridge and the meeting point of the Golden Horn, Bosphorus and Sea of Marmara. In the background is the Asian shore.

▼ Santa Sophia, or *Aya Sofya*, was built as a church in the sixth century A.D. by the Byzantine emperor Justinian. It was converted to a mosque by the Turks in 1453. Now it is a museum.

▲ Night view across Istanbul showing the Golden Horn with the Bosphorus and the Asian shore in the distance. Istanbul spans two continents, Europe and Asia, and has been called the world's oldest crossroads.

Arts ancient and modern

▼ Sixteenth century Iznik tiles in the Harem of Topkapi Palace, Istanbul. Beautiful ceramics were among the Ottoman artistic achievements. The finest are in the Blue Mosque in Istanbul and the Green Mosque in Bursa.

Influences from many cultures

Much of Turkish art comes originally from central Asia or is connected with the religion of Islam. Some of the designs of Turkish carpets are said to be Chinese. The great Ottoman mosques were of course religious architecture.

Turkish architecture was unlike either Persian or Greek. The greatest Turkish architect was Sinan (1489-1580), who designed masterpieces such as the Suleymaniye Mosque in Istanbul, and the Selimiye Mosque in Adrianople. Sinan lived to the age of 91, and constructed more than 400 buildings.

Some of the finest Turkish art is that of the Seljuk Turks, which is to be seen, not in Istanbul, but in Anatolia, in such towns as Konya, Sivas, and Erzurum. Seljuk art was more influenced by Persia than was the Ottoman art. There are wonderful Seljuk mosques, gateways, caravanserays (old

▼ The Blue Mosque in Istanbul. The name comes from the wonderful blue glazed tiles of the interior. This is perhaps the masterpiece of Turkish architecture.

▶ Part of the interior of Santa Sophia, showing the designs of calligraphy in the old Arabic script used in Turkey until the time of Atatürk.

wayside inns), and other buildings.

In Turkey there is also a great deal of art left over from peoples who lived in Anatolia before the arrival of the Turks, such as the Hittites, Greeks. Romans and Armenians.

Ceramics and calligraphy

Turkish ceramics have always been outstanding, and can be seen at their best in the famous Blue Mosque in Istanbul, or the superb tiles of Iznik. Calligraphy (ornamental writing), was always widely practised by the Turks, who were proficient in 160 different styles of writing. This was done in the Arabic script, with decorations known as "Arabesques".

Modern Turkish literature, painting and music flourishes in many forms. Turkey's best known writer is Yashar Kemal, who was proposed for the Nobel literature prize. He is author of "*Memed, My Hawk*", and many other novels.

Some leaders in the arts

▶ Turkey's best known writer, Yashar Kemal, is a large friendly man like a human bear.

♫ Idil Biret, Turkish pianist, has performed at home and abroad.

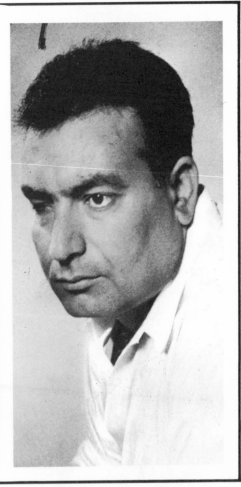

▼ Turkey carpets, as well known to the world as Persian carpets, are made on hand looms by women trained from childhood in this ancient art. The rich colours and intricate patterns differ slightly in each carpet, but each symbol used in the design has a meaning. This art was brought to Turkey by the first Turks.

Crossroads of the world

Before the Turks settled Turkey

The country which is today called Turkey —that is roughly speaking the old Asia Minor—was only taken over by the Turks after the eleventh century A.D., about 900 years ago. But the known history of Asia Minor goes back about 4,000 years. This means, of course, that the country was lived in by many races and peoples before the Turks arrived. Some of these created important civilizations. The history of Asia Minor is extraordinarily complicated.

The first empire in Anatolia was that of the Hittites, which lasted 500 years from 1700 to 1200 B.C. They were a strong soldierly people who achieved a high level of civilization and left carvings and a script. Their capital was at Hattusas, just east of Ankara. Troy also flourished until defeated by the Ancient Greeks around 1200 B.C. This war has become part of the world's cultural heritage, through Homer's great epics, the *Iliad* and *Odyssey*.

After the collapse of the Hittites, various lesser kingdoms were set up, of which the two most important were Phrygia (eighth century B.C.), and Lydia (seventh century). Lydia had its capital at Sardis, near the west coast of Anatolia. One king of Lydia was Croesus, the richest man of his time. Lydia was defeated by Persia, which occupied the whole of Anatolia in the fifth century B.C.

Alexander the Great

In 334 B.C. came Alexander the Great, from Macedonia in the West. He conquered Anatolia from the Persians, and brought with him the Greek culture. This began what is called the "Hellenization" of Asia Minor. Then, after 100 B.C., Anatolia became part of the Roman empire, and was almost completely Christianized by the two famous Christian apostles, St. Paul and Barnabas.

After the seventh century A.D. Anatolia was part of the Byzantine empire, ruled from Constantinople, today's Istanbul. It was the Byzantines who were defeated by the Seljuk Turks in 1071.

Earlier civilizations in Turkey

▼ Anatolia had an ancient and rich history long before the Seljuks made it a Turkish land. Early prehistoric settlements date back to 6000 B.C., and many civilizations flourished in Thrace and Anatolia before the Turks arrived there.

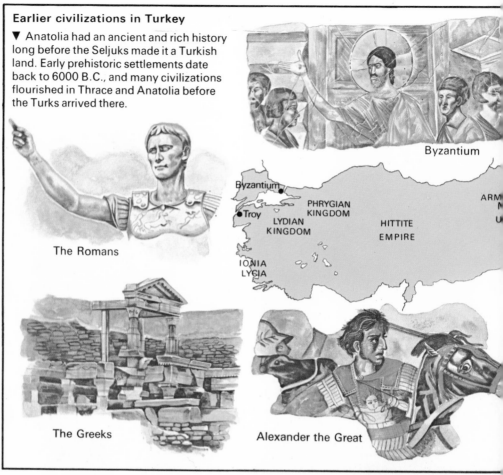

The Romans

Byzantium

The Greeks

Alexander the Great

▼ One of the best known Hittite rock carvings is this relief of running men. The Hittites also built thick-walled palaces, and made delicate gold and copper figures of animals and gods. At its height, the Hittite empire challenged the mighty empire of Rameses II in Egypt.

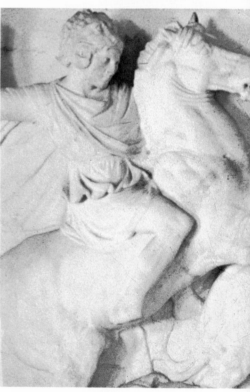

▲ Alexander the Great, the young Macedonian king, swept across Asia Minor with his armies. He crossed the Dardanelles in 334 B.C. and marched eastwards. His conquests reached east as far as India, but his empire soon crumbled.

The Hittites

Noah's Ark

The Persians

▼ Lycian tombs, carved out of the cliff face (seventh century B.C.). The Lycian kingdom had its capital at Phellos, near the south Mediterranean coast. Lycian rock tombs are found in great abundance here.

▲ A statue of Diana the Huntress, from the Roman period in Ephesus. There are many Roman remains in this area, including the ruins of the Basilica of St. John.

► Christ raising the dead. This mural painting of the Anastasis is in the Kariye Mosque, Istanbul. Byzantium, the capital of the eastern Roman empire, dates from the establishment of Christianity in Anatolia during the fourth century A.D.

The Seljuk Turks

▼ The Seljuk empire, at its greatest extent, stretched eastwards far beyond the borders of the Turkey of today.

The Seljuk Empire

BLACK SEA

CASPIAN SEA

TURKEY

MEDITERRANEAN SEA

PERSIAN GULF

RED SEA

Seljuk empire

The first Turkish empire

The first Turks to come out of Asia into Asia Minor were the Seljuks, so-called because they were descendants of a Turkish prince in Asia called Seljuk. These Seljuks defeated the Byzantines át the battle of Malazgirt, in eastern Anatolia, in 1071, and then created a large empire in the Middle East which included Persia, Iraq, Syria, and most of Anatolia. They were Muslims, and aroused the fears of the Christian West. It was mainly against the Seljuks that the Crusades were fought.

The Seljuk empire was less great than the Ottoman empire which came later: it lasted less than 200 years, as compared to the 600 years of the Ottoman empire, and was never so big or so strong. But the Seljuks were more civilized and more artistic than the Ottomans. Some of the finest Turkish architecture to be seen today is in or around the former Seljuk capital of Konya.

The Seljuks were ardent Muslims, and much of their art was religious. It was also

▼ An artist's impression of the crucial battle of Malazgirt in summer 1071, when the Seljuk Turks defeated the Byzantine armies of Emperor Romanus IV. This victory opened up the whole of Asia Minor to Turkish occupation.

very much influenced by Persia. The greatest literary figure of the Seljuk period was Jelaluddin Rumi, a poet and mystic who founded the religious order of the Mevlevi, better known to us as the "Whirling Dervishes". Performances of the Whirling Dervishes can still be seen today in Konya, the old Seljuk capital. It is a mystical religious rite, performed to music—very strange and beautiful.

Caravan routes

One characteristic of the Seljuk empire was the great encouragement it gave to commerce. At this period Anatolia was crisscrossed by countless caravan routes. Some of the finest Seljuk buildings were *caravansarays*, hotels or wayside inns on the trade routes. Many of these still stand today.

The Seljuk empire reached its most brilliant period under the Sultan Alaettin Kaikobad (1219-37). But soon after this, in 1243, the empire was overwhelmed by the Mongols, who emerged like a whirlwind from Asia conquering all in their path.

▲ Baldwin, Count of Flanders, storming the battlements of Constantinople during the Fourth Crusade, in 1204. The Crusades in Anatolia were fought mainly against the Seljuk Turks.

▼ Castle at Anamur on the south coast of Turkey. This magnificent medieval castle was probably built during the period of the Seljuk empire, but is sometimes attributed to the Armenians.

▲ A large Seljuk caravanseray at Sultan Han in central Anatolia. Caravanserays were rather like wayside inns on the trade routes. Notice the typical Seljuk gateway with its pointed arch.

▲ Interior of the Rose Garden Mosque in Kayseri, central Anatolia, showing the niche which faces Mecca (Mihrab), and tile work dating from the early thirteenth century, the finest of the Seljuk period.

▶ Painting of the Mongol emperor Genghis Khan receiving a deputation. The Mongul hordes defeated the Seljuks in 1243.

The mighty Ottomans

battle by a series of brilliant sultans with resounding titles such as Mahomet the Conqueror (who captured Istanbul in 1453 A.D.), Suleyman the Magnificent, Bayazid the Thunderbolt, and others.

The "terrible Turk"

The Ottoman advance terrified the West because it seemed the Turks would conquer the whole of Europe. A series of anti-Turkish drives were organized by Christian leaders. Martin Luther, the Protestant reformer, called for a struggle against "the world, the flesh, the Turk and the Devil". Men talked of the "terrible Turk". But twice the Turks failed to capture the city of Vienna; then in 1571 a great coalition, led by Don John of Austria, defeated the Turkish navy at the battle of Lepanto, near Corinth. From the seventeenth century onwards the mighty empire started to decline.

The old fear of the Turks led to anti-Turkish feeling in Europe. Yet study of the Ottoman empire shows that it was a much more liberal regime than foreigners thought. Admittedly the Sultan was an autocrat, but there was more religious toleration and opportunity for advancement by merit than existed in any European country at the time.

In the last 200 years of its existence the empire became so decadent that it was known as "the Sick Man of Europe". It finally collapsed in 1918, at the end of the First World War.

Conquerors for Islam

The Ottoman Empire lasted for more than 600 years, from about 1300 A.D. to 1918, and was one of the most brilliant and formidable empires in the history of the world.

The Ottoman state (the name comes from Osman or Othman, its first ruler) started as a tiny Turkish principality in north-west Anatolia, and expanded by force of armed conquest till at its height it stretched from Austria to the Persian Gulf in one direction, and from North Africa to central Asia in the other.

The force behind this terrific expansion was the religion of Islam. The Ottoman Turks were *Ghazis*, that is warriors for the Faith, conducting a Holy War against the "Infidel" (the Christians). They were led in

▲ Constantinople was besieged by the Turkish Sultan Mahomet II in 1453 and eventually captured. The capture of the city by the Turks had a profound effect on the world. For the Ottoman Turks, it was the achievement of one of their most cherished ambitions. Constantinople, renamed Istanbul, has been a Turkish city ever since.

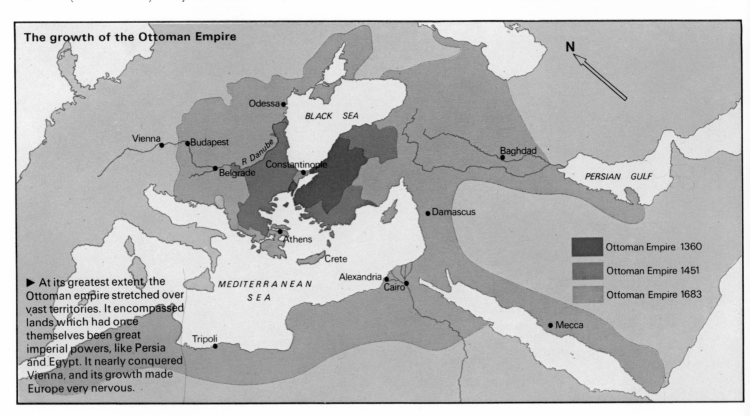

The growth of the Ottoman Empire

Odessa
BLACK SEA
Vienna
Budapest
R Danube
Belgrade
Constantinople
Baghdad
PERSIAN GULF
Damascus
Athens
Crete
Alexandria
MEDITERRANEAN SEA
Cairo
Tripoli
Mecca

Ottoman Empire 1360
Ottoman Empire 1451
Ottoman Empire 1683

► At its greatest extent, the Ottoman empire stretched over vast territories. It encompassed lands which had once themselves been great imperial powers, like Persia and Egypt. It nearly conquered Vienna, and its growth made Europe very nervous.

▲ The band of the Janissaries marching today, the ceremonial descendants of the famous infantry corps of the Ottoman empire. The Janissaries deposed several sultans, but were themselves destroyed by Sultan Mahmud II in 1826.

▶ A miniature showing Suleyman the Magnificent hawking. Hawking and hunting were favourite sports of the sultans, in the intervals of fighting battles or dallying in the harem.

▼ A contemporary Italian engraving of the Battle of Lepanto (1571) in which the Turkish navy was defeated by a coalition led by Don John of Austria. This defeat changed the Ottoman fortunes, and gave enemies in the West new confidence.

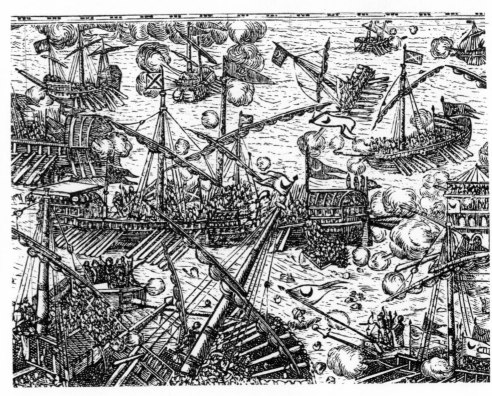

▲ A Turkish painting of the funeral of the Ottoman Sultan Suleyman the Magnificent. Suleyman was one of the greatest of the sultans and carried the empire to its widest extent. He is known to the Turks as ''Suleyman the Lawgiver''

Atatürk father of the Turks

The great soldier and statesman

Mustafa Kemal Atatürk (1881-1938) was one of the outstanding figures of history, being the rare combination of a brilliant military commander and a far-seeing statesman and reformer.

He influenced Turkish history in two ways. At the end of the First World War, Turkey had been crushingly defeated by the Allies, and invaded by a Greek army. Atatürk inspired the Turks to fight back and drive out the invaders. Thus he preserved his country's independence.

Secondly he embarked on an extraordinary series of radical reforms designed to change Turkey from the oriental despotism of the Sultans into a modern democratic state, with trade, cultural and diplomatic links with the West. He abolished the Sultanate and became first president of a new Turkish Republic in 1923.

Atatürk was determined to counteract the conservative influence of Islam. He believed the people's religion made them fatalistic, prepared to accept bad conditions in society. To a large extent he separated Turkey from Islam, which had been the Turks' religion for centuries, by making Turkey a "secular" state.

The effect of these reforms was to change the old oriental image of Turkey, and bring the country into much closer harmony with Europe and the West.

Atatürk made the Turks wear European hats instead of turbans and fezzes. He also compelled people to adopt surnames. One of his most important reforms was to adopt the European script in 1928. He himself travelled all over Turkey teaching the peasants to read and write.

Hero-worship

Atatürk was a man of heroic vigour, of whom it was said that he quivered with energy even when he was sitting still. He inspired the Turkish people to an extraordinary pitch of hero-worship. He adopted the unique name of Atatürk—"Father of the Turks", and is always known in Turkey as the "Eternal Leader".

◀ Mustafa Kemal (later he adopted the surname Atatürk). At the time this famous photograph was taken, he was Commander-in-Chief of the Turkish Nationalist forces in the War of Independence 1919-22.

◀ Allied troops landing in Anzac Bay on the Gallipoli Peninsula during the Dardanelles Campaign in 1915. Due largely to Mustafa Kemal's leadership, the Turks repulsed the allied landings and prevented the capture of Constantinople, thus influencing the course of the war.

▼ Statues of women mourning the death of Atatürk. The picture, taken at dawn, shows Atatürk's mausoleum at Ankara in the background. It is in the form of a colonnaded temple.

▲ Atatürk teaching the European alphabet to peasants in a Turkish village. He went all over Turkey teaching after he decided to make Turkey adopt the Western (Roman) script in place of the Arabic script in 1928.

▼ Kizilay junction, the central point of modern Ankara. Atatürk made it the capital, in place of Istanbul, when he founded the Turkish republic in 1923. Ankara was then a sleepy little provincial town.

▲ Mustafa Kemal (left) at the battle of Kocatepe during the war of Independence against the Greeks (1922). This war was one of the critical conflicts of modern history, because it prevented a Greek occupation of Asia Minor and established it as an independent Turkish land.

45

Language and the media

A major world language

The Turkish language is quite different from Arabic or Persian or any of the Indo-European languages. It belongs to the Uralo-Altaic linguistic group, which includes Finnish, Hungarian and Estonian, and is very difficult for a Westerner to learn.

Turkish is what is called an "agglutinative" language, which means that suffixes are added on to the stems of words to produce many subtle shades of meaning. This often causes words of enormous length.

Though Turkish has a grammar and sound which seems strange to people speaking Indo-European languages like English, it is a language which is spoken right through the middle of Asia. Travelling overland from Bulgaria to China, you could use it all the way.

The Turkish press and modern Turkish writers try to avoid long words and use more simple Turkish. There are many excellent Turkish columnists who write in a very effective pungent style.

Newspapers and T.V.

There is an enormous number of newspapers and magazines in Turkey, about 700 altogether. Some of these are scurrilous and of a high standard. The two best are *Milliyet* and *Cumhuriyet*, both published in Istanbul. The total circulation of the press is about 4 million.

Broadcasting in Turkey comes under a monopoly of the Turkish Radiö and T.V. Corporation, which is governed by the Constitution. It is modelled to some extent on the B.B.C., and like its British model, is supposed to be impartial between the various political parties. Whether it succeeds or not is a matter of endless argument in coffee bars. Television has only started recently, but is being expanded to cover the country.

▲ Shop advertisement signs in a narrow street, showing a confusion of Turkish and Western product names.

Some aspects of the Turkish language

▶ Teşkilatlandirilamiyacaklarindandir means "it is due to the fact that it will not be possible for them to be organized". Seventeen words of English become one word in Turkish.

▲ "Yok" is the Turkish negative, and is a word all foreigners learn, however short a time they spend in Turkey. Turks usually say the word with an upward movement of the head, which can be very irritating.

▼ The Turks have many picturesque ways of expressing things. "When fishes climb the poplar trees" is the idiomatic way of saying "it will never happen".

▲ There are vast numbers of newspapers and magazines in Turkey. A few are good, but many are vulgar and trashy. International magazines can also be bought.

▲ Scene from the film *Dubious Patriots*. This film was made by an American company, with a mixed Turkish and American cast. The Turkish cinema industry is enterprising and prolific.

▶ A television joke, on a modern world theme, from the Turkish newspaper, *Milliyet*. Television, still new in Turkey, is expanding fast, but radio is the most important way of spreading the news.

How the Turks see themselves

How a Turk might see the national character

▲ Turks are dignified, not always very communicative, and often too proud to be commercially minded.

▲ Turks are natural aristocrats, and love things to be big and imposing. But for "petty" details, like maintenance, they have little time.

The natural aristocrats

Turks like to think of themselves as a Mediterranean people, though in truth they are not really Mediterranean in character. They are too dignified, not talkative enough, and not interested enough in making money. They are too proud to be commercially-minded.

Like other Turanian races, such as the Hungarians and Finns, the Turks are natural aristocrats. In their whole history they have never been ruled over or colonized by any other nation. Rather it was they who ruled over Greeks, Arabs, Bulgarians, and so on, who were part of the Ottoman empire. Even today the Turks have a slightly patronising manner towards these former subject peoples.

Curious mixture

Turks are a curious mixture, because along with their pride and self-confidence they also feel a deep need to be flattered and reassured that everything in their country

▲ Turks like to know that what they make is admired. "Güzel!" means "beautiful" and is a reassuring word to hear.

meets the standards of foreigners. Visitors to Turkey have constantly to be saying the Turkish word "Güzel!", meaning "Beautiful!".

They love starting things off in a grandiose way, but are not always so good at maintaining their grand constructions. They tend not to bother about repairs. This is because in the Ottoman empire things like this were left to so-called "inferior" peoples like the Armenians or Greeks. The Turks did the ruling and fighting.

The Turks respect the British, partly because the British once had as big an empire as they had. During the First World War, the Turks and British were fighting on opposite sides, yet many British soldiers returned from Gallipoli with reports that "Johnny Turk" made a brave soldier.

Turks are sincere, dignified, extremely honourable, and immensely hospitable. They rate friendship very highly. If you have a Turkish friend, you have a friend for life.

▲ Sometimes Turks will be most disparaging about other people's creations, but their own *must* be admired.

▲ Like other peoples who have once had great imperial power, Turks are sometimes somewhat disdainful of people belonging to former subject nations.

48

▼ Wreaths laid at a war memorial in Istanbul. The Turks are a martial and patriotic people, and are brave fighters in war.

▲ Turks often gather in the market place to talk. Men congregate in the coffee bars, but women must break off from their shopping to talk.

◄ Turkish peasant on donkey in Cappadocia, central Anatolia. Donkeys are a very typical sight in the Turkish countryside, particularly on the Anatolian plateau.

▲ Turkish peasants are famous for their hospitality. Here a peasant family is entertaining a foreigner to a meal in their small, neat cottage.

The Turkish influence

Turkey and the world

Certain well-known Turkish products and institutions have gone all over the world, such as Turkish baths, coffee, cigarettes, and towels, or Turkish Delight and Turkey carpets. But the Turkish influence on world history has been more profound.

Such historic events and episodes as the Crusades, the Renaissance, the discovery of America and of the Cape route to India have been partly due to Turkish power.

For example, when the Seljuk Turks conquered Anatolia, and Islam spread across Palestine, Christian Europe sent its Crusaders in an attempt to capture the Middle East from the Turks and Arabs. The Crusaders met civilizations in many ways more advanced than their own, and came back with new knowledge which revived interest in the arts and sciences.

Then when the Turks, in turn, captured Constantinople, many scholars fled to Rome taking with them ancient Greek manuscripts. These helped revive the neglected learning of classical times, and the Renaissance was partly due to these discoveries.

Western European explorers began to travel south and west, because the Turks cut off the land route to India and China. Thus, indirectly, the Turks contributed to the voyages of discovery.

The Turkish empire

The Turkish empire, at its greatest extent, stretched nearly to Vienna, and south across Egypt and the whole coastline of North Africa. The Ottoman Turks were devout Muslims, and though they allowed religious tolerance during their 600 years of empire, countries they ruled absorbed much of Turkish religion and culture.

Turkey today is politically allied with the West in the North Atlantic Treaty Organization (N.A.T.O.). Turkey has, however, remained on friendly terms with the Soviet countries. Turkey is of great strategic importance, because of her position in the Eastern Mediterranean, and she controls the outlets from the Black Sea.

▲ A medieval print showing the siege of Constantinople by the Turks in 1453. The Turkish capture of the city had profound effects in the West.

▶ Barbarossa came from a family of notorious pirates who pillaged the coasts of Italy and Spain. Suleyman the Magnificent, the Ottoman emperor, made him his Grand Admiral, and this seasoned freebooter won many battles and much treasure for Suleyman. Barbarossa was one of the fighting men who increased Turkish might.

▼ The battle of Navarino in 1827. In this battle the combined fleets of Britain, France and Russia annihilated Turkish naval power; Turkey's power declined after this time.

▲ A squad of Turkish troops on parade in Ankara. Turkey is the strongest military power in the Middle East. Turkish might, which once won a vast empire, is now allied with the West in the North Atlantic Treaty Organization (N.A.T.O.).

▼ The bedroom of Sultan Murad III in the Harem of Topkapi Palace. The walls show Ottoman calligraphy (Arabic writing) and ceramics, two arts in which the Turks have excelled. Turkey has also contributed to architecture and literature.

Some Turkish gifts to the world

▲ Turkish coffee, cigarettes and fruit, Turkish delight and Meerschaum pipes are among luxury products which come from Turkey.

▲ The Turkish bath is a Turkish institution which is well known in many parts of the world.

◀ "Turkey" carpets and Turkish towels are a household word in many countries. Turks are talented weavers.

51

New Directions

The changing face of Turkey

There are still many signs of the old Turkey left, in the bazaars, the *hammams*, the dress of the peasant women, the camels, and so on. But Atatürk not only changed the appearance of things, he opened the doors to political and economic development. After Atatürk's death in 1938, Ismet Inönü became President. He introduced a regime of full parliamentary democracy on the western model. With one interlude of 17 months in 1960-61, when the Army took over, democracy has lasted to the present day.

In Turkey, as in any rapidly changing society, there are serious political tensions. Furthermore, Turkey's position in the Eastern Mediterranean, gives it great strategical importance in a troubled area of the globe. Turkey is also very near to the big oil producing states. Istanbul commands the outlet from the Black Sea, and is thus very important to the Soviet Union, because all Soviet shipping from its southern ports has to pass through the Bosphorus. So the big powers have an interest in Turkey's friendship, and the United States has provided $3,500 million in aid since 1950. Germany has also invested heavily in Turkey. Industry has boomed, and Turkey is becoming a more urban society. In 1955 peasants formed 80 per cent of the population; by 1974 the proportion had declined to 65 per cent.

The invasion of Cyprus

Turkey is also troubled by the unresolved problem of Cyprus. This Mediterranean island, with Greek and Turkish inhabitants, has inflamed the old hostilities between Greece and Turkey. Turkey invaded the island in late 1974 and the two nations very nearly came to open warfare.

The rapid population growth, and serious inflation, have caused high unemployment in the towns at a period when young Turks cannot always rely on earning high wages in Germany. None the less, the future looks bright: Turkey's mineral wealth provides excellent potential, and the foundations of a dynamic society, so well laid by Atatürk, have supported Turkey through many crises.

▲ Tourism is an important new industry in Turkey, which provides the country with valuable foreign exchange. Holidaymakers are attracted by Turkey's history, and its superb, uncrowded beaches.

▲ These Turkish workers are waiting their turn for a medical examination in Istanbul, before taking up a two-year contract to work in Germany. Many Turks work abroad, and bring back their savings.

▲ A Coca-cola stand outside the main station in Istanbul, an example of the impact of the United States. The Turkish words on the front of the stall mean "the real taste of life".

▲ The oil refinery at Batman in south-east Turkey is an example of the modern industrial plant being introduced. Turkey's oil resources are probably not large, but they should reduce the imports bill.

◀ Tractors queuing at a weighing station. Turkish agriculture has advanced greatly, producing higher yields. Mechanization, particularly the use of tractors, has provided great benefits to farming.

▲ Turkish soldiers in action near Famagusta in the 1974 invasion of Cyprus. Cyprus belonged to Turkey for 300 years and many Turks still think of it as a Turkish island, although Greeks outnumber Turks.

Reference
Human and physical geography

The climate of Turkey

Turkey as a whole lies in the temperate zone, though its climate has considerable regional variations. The south has a typical Mediterranean climate, which is felt on the Aegean (west) coast and up to

markedly more northerly climate. The Black Sea coast has a milder sea climate than the other coastal areas. In Central Anatolia summers are dry and hot, and the winters cold, with frequent snowfalls. In mountainous eastern Anatolia the summers are cool, but winter is severe. South-eastern Anatolia has hot dry summers and mild winters. The eastern end of the Black Sea coast has high rainfall.

LAND AND PEOPLE
Full title: Republic of Turkey.
Position: Between 26 and 45 E and 36 and 45 N. Straddles Europe and Asia.
Constituent parts: Anatolia (roughly old "Asia Minor") and Thrace (formerly "Turkey in Europe").
Area: 780,576 sq. km. (301,380 sq. miles)
Population: about 40 million
Flag: white star and crescent on red background
Anthem: "Independence March": "Fear not, be not dismayed"
Language: Turkish
Religion: 99% Muslim
Capital: Ankara. Pop. 1,603,125
The State: Republic since 1923. New constitution 1961. Amended 1971
Political system: parliamentary democracy
Armed forces: Army 400,000; Navy 40,000; Airforce 50,000 (1972)
International Organizations: Turkey belongs to U.N., N.A.T.O., C.E.N.T.O., O.E.C.D., and Council of Europe, Associate Member of E.E.C.

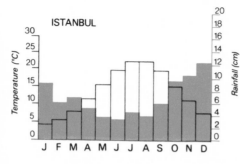

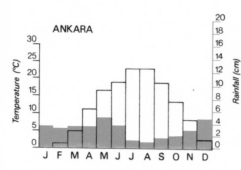

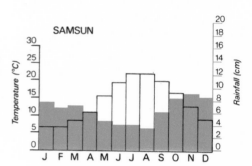

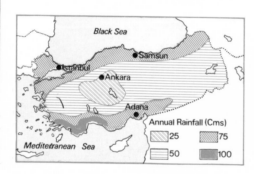

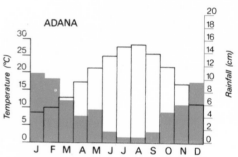

The natural vegetation of Turkey

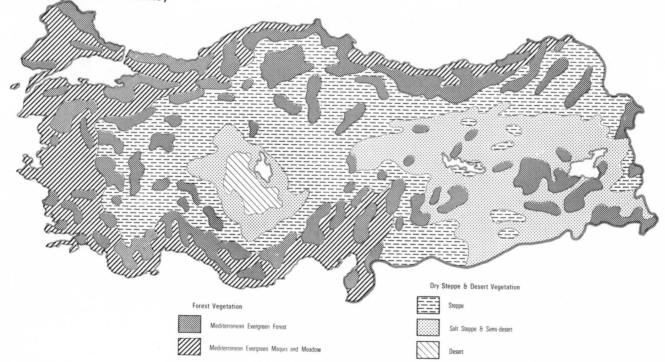

Forest Vegetation
- Mediterranean Evergreen Forest
- Mediterranean Evergreen Maquis and Meadow

Dry Steppe & Desert Vegetation
- Steppe
- Salt Steppe & Semi-desert
- Desert

The population density

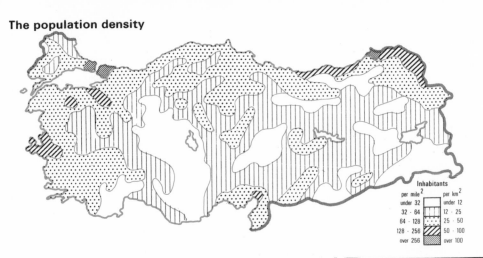

Inhabitants	
per mile²	per km²
under 32	under 12
32 - 64	12 - 25
64 - 128	25 - 50
128 - 256	50 - 100
over 256	over 100

◀ The population of Turkey was 39,348,000 in 1974. There is an average density of 50 inhabitants per km². The rate of population increase, at 2.5% per year, is one of the world's highest. The population explosion has caused a great strain on all resources, such as education, health services, housing, water, energy and transport.

The emigration of some 700,000 Turkish workers to western Europe (mainly West Germany) in recent years has done little to alleviate the problem. One of the main features of Turkey's population increase has been the drift of peasants to the cities. Family planning has not yet made much progress.

Population of principal towns

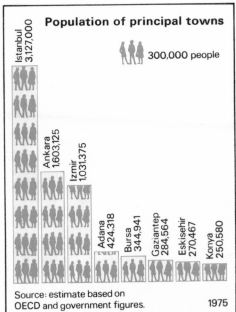

👫 300,000 people

Istanbul 3,127,000
Ankara 1,603,125
Izmir 1,031,375
Adana 424,318
Bursa 344,941
Gaziantep 284,564
Eskisehir 270,467
Konya 250,580

Source: estimate based on OECD and government figures.
1975

▶ Turkey is a parliamentary democracy in which the legislative power is exercised by a two-chamber parliament called the Grand National Assembly. This is composed of the National Assembly (lower house) and Senate (upper house). The National Assembly consists of 450 members elected by universal suffrage for a 4-year term. The Senate is composed of 150 members plus 15 senators appointed by the President of the Republic and certain other life-members, making about 187 senators in all.

The executive power is vested in the President of the Republic, who is elected for a 7-year term and is a non-party head of state. The President appoints the Prime Minister, who in turn nominates his government.

The judiciary consists of a Court of Appeal, a Council of State (for administrative cases), a Court of Military Appeal, and a Supreme Council of Judges which deals with all judicial appointments. There is also a Constitutional Court which decides whether laws passed by Parliament are constitutional or not.

The system of Government

Supreme Council of Judges

Constitutional court

President, elected head of state

Senate

Prime Minister

Cabinet

National Assembly 450 members

The electorate

Reference
History

MAIN EVENTS IN TURKISH HISTORY
THE SELJUKS
A.D.

1071   Seljuk Turks from central Asia defeat Byzantine empire at Battle of Malazgirt

1097   Crusades begin. Partly aimed to recapture Asia Minor from Turks

Seljuks and Crusaders in battle

1100-1250   Turks gradually take over Anatolia. Seljuk empire set up with capital at Konya

1243   Mongol invasions of Anatolia destroy Seljuk power

RISE OF OTTOMAN POWER

1280   Rise of Ottoman Turkish emirate in north-west Anatolia

1326   Ottoman Turks capture Brusa (Bursa) which becomes Turkish capital

1362   Turks conquer Thrace

1389   Turks overthrow Serbia

1393   Turks overrun Bulgaria

1438   Foundation of corps of Janissaries

1453   Turks capture Constantinople and make it Ottoman capital

1463   Turkish conquest of Bosnia

1492   Columbus discovers New World

1494   Portuguese navigators reach India by Cape route

ZENITH OF OTTOMAN POWER

1516-17   Turks conquer Syria and Egypt

1520-66   Sultanate of Suleyman the Magnificent

1521   Suleyman captures Belgrade

1526   Turks defeat Hungary

1529   First unsuccessful Turkish siege of Vienna

1570   Turks capture Cyprus

1571   Turks defeated at naval battle of Lepanto by coalition led by Don John of Austria

1574   Turks capture Tunis

1683   Second unsuccessful Turkish siege of Vienna

1687   Turks driven out of Hungary and Serbia

DECLINE OF OTTOMAN EMPIRE

1682-1725   Reign of Peter the Great in Russia starts new period of Russo-Turkish rivalry. Peter conquers Crimea, from Turkey

1718   Ottomans cede territory to Austria

1768-74   Russo-Turkish war gives Russia right to pass through the Straits

1788   War breaks out between Ottoman Empire and Austro-Russian coalition

1789-1807   French Revolution gives Turks breathing-space

1802   Peace Treaty between Ottoman Empire and France

1807   Sultan Selim III deposed by revolt of Janissaries

1808-39   Reign of "westernizing" Sultan Mahmud II

1826   Mahmud II suppresses Janissaries

1828   Mahmud replaces turban by fez as Turkish headgear

1839   Thoroughgoing legal, financial and administrative reform of the Ottoman state undertaken by Mahmud II, and his son Abdulmejid, known as the *Tanzimat,* (Reorganization)

1854-6   Crimean War. Ottoman Empire supported by Britain and France against Russia

1870-76   War with Russia

1878   Under Treaty of San Stefano, Turks lose Roumania, Serbia,

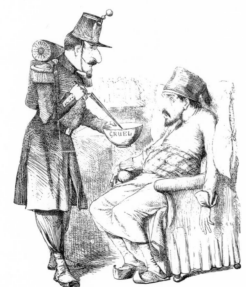

The ' Sick Man of Europe''

Montenegro and Bulgaria. Britain occupies Cyprus. Ottoman Empire starts to break up. Turkey known as the "Sick Man of Europe"

1908   Young Turk revolution deposes Sultan Abdul Hamid II. Turkey governed by "Committee of Union and Progress" headed by Enver Pasha

1914   Turkey enters First World War on German side

1915   Gallipoli campaign. Turks repulse Allied landings

1917-18   Turks lose Arabia, Palestine and the rest of their empire in Middle East. Constantinople occupied by Allied troops. Greeks land in Smyrna (Izmir). Treaty of Sèvres tries to carve up Turkey

ATATÜRK AND INDEPENDENCE

1919   Mustafa Kemal lands at Turkish Black Sea port of Samsun. Greek army starts to occupy Western Anatolia

1921   Mustafa Kemal decisively defeats Greeks at Battle of Sakarya and saves Turkey

1923   Treaty of Lausanne restores Turkey's 1914 frontiers. Foundation of Turkish Republic. Atatürk declared first President

1924   Abolition of Muslim Caliphate

1924-38   Atatürk's reforms make Turkey a modern state

1938   Death of Atatürk. Succeeded as President by Ismet Inönü

1939-45   Turkey maintains neutrality in Second World War

1945   President Inönü introduces democracy

1950   Inönü and Republican People's party defeated in first free election in Turkish history. Adnan Menderes and Democrat party take power

1960   Menderes overthrown by army coup

1961   Menderes tried and executed. Army restores parliamentary government

1965   Demirel and Justice party win general elections.

1971   Demirel resigns after intervention by Army

1973   New elections won by Republican Peoples party. Bulent Ecevit becomes Prime Minister

1974   Turkey intervenes in Cyprus after pro-Greek coup and occupies part of island.

1975   Turkey supports declaration of autonomous Turkish-Cypriot zone in northern Cyprus Turkish takeover of all U.S. military bases in Turkey.

THE LIFE OF ATATÜRK

1881 Birth of Mustafa in Salonika, Greece, at that time part of Ottoman Empire

1893 Mustafa enters military secondary school at Salonika, where he is given additional name of Kemal

1899 Mustafa Kemal enters War College in Constantinople

1907 Captain Kemal posted to 3rd Army in Salonika

1908 Young Turk Revolution forces Sultan Abdul Hamid to restore constitution

1909 Counter-revolution in Constantinople. Deposition and exile of Abdul Hamid

1912 First Balkan War. Serbia Bulgaria and Greece invade Turkey. Kemal appointed Director of Operations in Adrianople

1913 Second Balkan War. Kemal appointed military attache in Sofia

1914 Turkey enters First World War on side of Germany

1915 Kemal appointed to command of 19th division in Thrace. Checks Allied landings at Gallipoli

1916 Kemal promoted General and Pasha

1917 Kemal appointed commander of 7th Army in Syria

1918 Armistice signed between Turkey and Britain at Mudros. Kemal returns to Constantinople

1919 Opening of Versailles Peace Conference. Kemal appointed Inspector-General of 9th Army in Anatolia and lands at Samsun on Black Sea coast. Kemal issues Declaration of Turkish Independence. Resigns from Army

1920 Greek Army advances into Anatolia, supported by British government

1921 Greek advance checked at first Battle of Inönü. Mustafa Kemal defeats Greeks at critical Battle of Sakarya. Kemal given title of *Gazi* by Turkish Grand National Assembly

1922 Turkish nationalist forces defeat Greeks and drive them into sea at Smyrna. Kemal abolishes Sultanate in Turkey

1923 Treaty of Lausanne establishes Turkey's independence. Proclamation of Turkish Republic with Kemal as first President

1925 Abolition of fez and suppression of Dervish orders in Turkey

1926 Turkey adopts Swiss Civil Code

1928 Turkey abolishes Arabic script and adopts Roman alphabet

1932 Turkey joins League of Nations

1934 First 5-year plan for Turkish industrial development. Mustafa Kemal takes name of "Atatürk" ("Father Turk"), and compels all Turks to take surnames

1936 Montreux Convention signed, giving Turkey control of the Straits. King Edward VIII visits Atatürk in Istanbul

1938 Death of Atatürk

The Arts

THE ARTS
LITERATURE

Mevlana Jelaluddin Rumi (1207-1273): poet and mystic of the Seljuk period. His chief work was the *Mathnavi* (or *Mesnevi*), a long and very sublime mystical poem. Founded the sect of the Mevlevi (Whirling Dervishes).

Yunus Emreh 13th century Anatolian folk poet and minstrel. Poems have a strong mystical content. Very popular. Pilgrimages made to his shrine.

Pir Sultan Abdal 16th century poet of dissident Alevi sect. Said to have taken part in an Alevi rebellion and been hanged by the Pasha of Sivas, in central Anatolia.

Ziya Pasha (1825-80) political writer and pioneer of western literature under the Ottoman Empire. Translated French literature into Turkish. Advocated democracy for Turkey following a dream he had when sleeping on a bench on Hampstead Heath, during a visit to London.

Ibrahim Sinasi (1826-71) political writer and "westernizer" under the Ottoman Empire.

Namik Kemal (1840-88) poet, philosopher, and apostle of political freedom for Turkey under tyrannical rule of Sultan Abdul Hamid II. Much influenced by French ideas, especially Rousseau and Montesquieu.

Ziya Gökalp (1876-1924) Turkish philosopher and sociologist who advocated Turkish nationalism during and after First World War. Very influential in Turkey. Some of his ideas were later put into practice by Atatürk.

Ömer Seyfettin Short story writer of the early days of the Turkish Republic. Noted for his clear and graceful prose.

Yahya Kemal Well-known Turkish poet under Republic, whose verse is often quoted.

Nazim Hikmet Probably best-known Turkish poet of 20th century. Was a Communist, and spent many years in prison. Died in 1963 in Moscow.

Yakup Kadri Karaosmanoglu Turkish novelist. His most famous book was *Yaban* ("The Stranger") 1930, which described the gulf between Turkish intellectuals and peasants in the 1920s. Died in 1974 at age of 88.

Halideh Edip Adivar Very well-known political writer who fought with Atatürk in Turkish War of Independence. She wrote partly in English. *The Turkish Ordeal.*

Sait Faik (1907-54) Modern Turkish short-story writer, famous for his tales about life in and around Istanbul. His stories have been translated into French.

Yashar Kemal (born 1922) Turkey's best known contemporary writer, whose books have been translated into many languages. In English the titles are *Memed, my Hawk, The Wind from the Plain, Anatolian Tales.*

Aziz Nesin Turkey's best-known modern satirist and humorous writer. Has written about 80 books.

Mahmut Makal Former peasant and schoolmaster who wrote a famous book about Turkish peasant life in 1950, called *Our Village.* Translated into many languages.

PAINTING AND SCULPTURE
Both these two arts were virtually forbidden in Ottoman Turkey because the religion of Islam did not permit representation of the human form. They were replaced to some extent by calligraphy and ceramic art, both of which flourished in Turkey. There are a number of modern Turkish painters and sculptors. Two of the best known are:

Bedri Rahmi Eyuboglu (born 1913) Also a ceramicist. One of his mosaic panels is to be seen in the United Nations building in New York.

Ibrahim Balaban Very original painter of mainly peasant themes. Has left-wing views and is often in prison.

ARCHITECTURE
Sinan (1489-1580) the most celebrated architect of the Ottoman period. Designed the Suleymaniye mosque in Istanbul, the Selimiye mosque in Adrianople, and many other mosques and secular buildings.

Emin Onat a distinguished contemporary architect. Designer of the Atatürk Mausoleum in Ankara, where the tomb of Atatürk is housed. This is frequently regarded as one of the finest of modern buildings.

MUSIC
Adnan Saygun (born 1907) modern Turkish composer. Oratorio *Yunus Emreh.*

Nevit Kodalli operas *Van Gogh* and *The Epic of Gilgamesh.*

Ilhan Uzmanbas modern Turkish exponent of the 12-tone scale.

CERAMICS
Fureya Koral is Turkey's leading modern exponent of this art. Her work has been exhibited in Paris and other European cities.

Reference
The Economy

FACTS AND FIGURES
Total wealth (1973)
£9,500 million. Per head: £227
Economic growth (1968-73)
7.1% per year
Main sources of income
Agriculture wheat, barley, maize, rye, tobacco, cotton, mohair, figs, nuts, grapes, citrus fruit, opium, olives. Cattle, buffalo, sheep and goats.
Mining coal, lignite, chrome ore, iron ore, copper, petroleum products. Hydro-electric power.
Industry woollen and cotton fabrics and yarns, cement, superphosphate, sugar, glass, paper, pig iron, steel ingots, sheets and pipes, coke, olive oil, electrical equipment, footwear, handicrafts. Tourism has rapidly developed in recent years.
Main trading partners Germany, Italy, E.E.C. countries, United Kingdom, E.F.T.A. countries, United States, Japan, Eastern bloc.
Currency 1 Turkish lira=100 kurush. £1=32 liras approximately (1975).

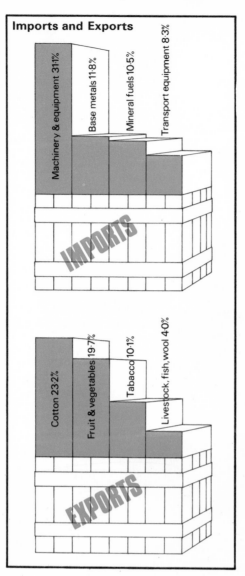

Imports and Exports

IMPORTS: Machinery & equipment 31.1% · Base metals 11.8% · Mineral fuels 10.5% · Transport equipment 8.3%

EXPORTS: Cotton 23.2% · Fruit & vegetables 19.7% · Tabacco 10.1% · Livestock, fish, wool 4.0%

◄ Turkey's main exports are tobacco, cotton, fruit and vegetables, hazelnuts, and other agricultural products, chrome ore, as well as a number of processed and manufactured products.

The main imports are coffee, livestock, textiles, fertilisers, chemical products, machinery and equipment, and minerals. Turkey's 5-year plans, which started in 1963, have been focussed mainly on increasing exports and stepping up goods which can lead to import substitution. With large numbers of Turks working in western Europe, mainly West Germany, there has been a spectacular rise in workers' remittances from abroad to help the Turkish balance of payments. Remittances increased from $471 million in 1971 to $1,200 million in 1973. Receipts from tourism are gradually improving ($78 million in 1973), but more development is needed.

Turkey has been hard hit by the rise in the price of crude oil. However, since 1971 exports of Turkish industrial products have risen strongly, reaching 31% of total exports in 1974.

▼ Turkey is still largely an agricultural country, with peasants forming about 65% of the total population. This figure is however, constantly diminishing with industrialization.

There has been a considerable increase in irrigation and the use of fertilizers in recent years, though Turkish cereal yields are still low compared with western Europe or the United States. "Dry farming", without rotation of crops, is still practised in Anatolia, and there are many small uneconomic farms.

Agriculture in Turkey

Wheat · Maize · Vegetables · Olives · Tobacco · Citrus Fruit · Camels · Barley · Rice · Sugar-beet · Grapes · Cotton · Goats

Industry in Turkey

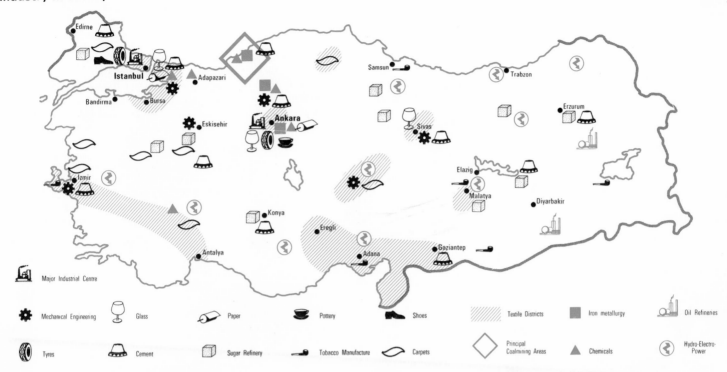

Symbol	Legend		Symbol	Legend
	Major Industrial Centre			Textile Districts
	Mechanical Engineering	Glass	Iron metallurgy	Oil Refineries
	Paper	Pottery	Shoes	
	Tyres	Cement	Sugar Refinery	Tobacco Manufacture	Carpets
	Principal Coalmining Areas	Chemicals	Hydro-Electro-Power

How Turkish people are employed

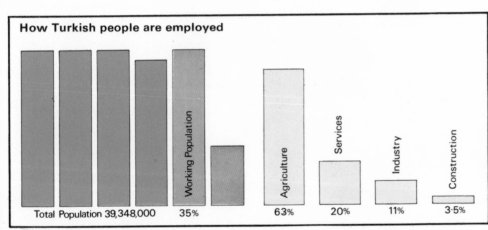

Total Population 39,348,000   35%   Working Population

Agriculture 63%   Services 20%   Industry 11%   Construction 3·5%

◀ The Turkish labour force totals about 14 million, of which 8.7 million are in agriculture, 1.6 million in industry, half a million in construction work, and 2.8 million in services. Unemployment stands officially at 1.7 million, but there is a considerable amount of disguised unemployment and under-employment. In recent years about 700,000 Turkish workers have emigrated to western Europe and this has slightly alleviated the problem.

Goods owned by the Turks, compared with other nations

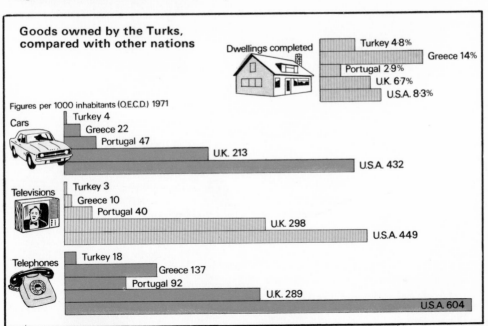

Dwellings completed   Turkey 4·8%   Greece 14%   Portugal 2·9%   U.K. 6·7%   U.S.A. 8·3%

Figures per 1000 inhabitants (O.E.C.D.) 1971

Cars
Turkey 4
Greece 22
Portugal 47
U.K. 213
U.S.A. 432

Televisions
Turkey 3
Greece 10
Portugal 40
U.K. 298
U.S.A. 449

Telephones
Turkey 18
Greece 137
Portugal 92
U.K. 289
U.S.A. 604

The problem of inflation

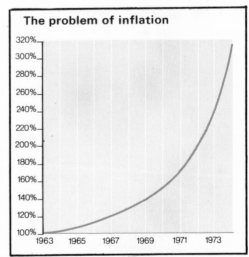

▲ As in many other countries inflation has been serious in Turkey, reaching a figure of about 35% in the first 5 months of 1974. This has affected Turkey's farmers and salary-earners, but the government's price policies and the trade unions have increased many real incomes.

Gazetteer

Adana (37 10N 35 18E) Pop. (1975) 424,318. Capital of Adana province, on Seyhan river. Industrial and commercial centre. Manufactures cotton goods, tobacco products. Trade in cereals, cotton. Ruins of Castle of Harun al-Rashid (782 A.D.). Stone bridge, partly dating from reign of Justinian.

Aegean Sea (38 0N 25 0E) Arm of the Mediterranean, between Greece and Turkey. Linked by the Dardanelles to the Sea of Marmara and Black Sea. Leading Turkish port is Izmir.

Anatolia (39 0N 32 30E) "Anadolu" in Turkish. Peninsula between Black Sea and Mediterranean. Greater part of Turkey. A high plateau, averaging 760 m. (2,500 ft.) Pontic Mountains in north, Taurus in south, merge in east to form the Armenian Knot. Highest point is Mt. Ararat. Many salt lakes. West and South coasts have Mediterranean climate. Taken by Ottoman Turks in 13th-14th centuries.

Ankara (39 58N 32 28E) Formerly "Angora". Pop. (1975) 1,603,125. Capital of Turkey since 1923, and capital of Ankara province. Commercial and industrial centre. Trade in grain, wool, mohair from local goats. Manufactures textiles, cement, leather goods. University (1946). Technical university (1956). Ancient temple with Monumentum Ancyranum. Atatürk Mausoleum. Captured by Tartars in 1402. Re-taken by Turks in 1415. Present city almost completely modern.

Antakya (36 10N 36 15E) Antioch. Pop. (1965) 57,000. Capital of Hatay province, on Orontes river. Commercial centre. Trade in grain, cotton. Founded c. 300 B.C. by Seleucus I. Early Christian centre. Captured by Persians A.D. 538; by Arabs 636; by Seljuks 1084; by Mamelukes 1268; by Ottoman Turks in 1516.

Ararat, Mount (39 40N 44 25E) *Agri Dagi.* Volcanic mountain in north-east near borders of Iran and Soviet Armenia. Two chief peaks: Little Ararat 3,900 m. (12,800 ft.) Great Ararat 5,180 m. (16,900 ft.). The Ark is said to have rested on the latter after Noah's Flood.

Black Sea (43 0N 34 0E) Ancient Euxine Sea. Inland sea bounded north and east by U.S.S.R.; in the south by Turkey; west by Bulgaria and Rumania. Connected to the Sea of Azov (in north-east) by the Kerch Strait. Connected with the Aegean and Mediterranean in south-west by the Bosphorus, Sea of Marmara, and the Dardanelles. East and south coasts mountainous; west and north low-lying with lagoons at river mouths. Receives many rivers, including Danube, Dniester, Dnieper, South Bug, Don. It has low salinity and is almost tideless. Outward surface flow to Bosphorus. Stagnant and lifeless below 80 fathoms. Fisheries.

Surrounded by Turkish territory in 15th-19th centuries.

Bosphorus (41 10N 29 6E) Ancient Bosporus Thracius. Also known as Bosporus. Name signifies "Ox-ford". *Karadeniz Bogazi* in Turkish. Strait between Asian and European Turkey, linking Black Sea and Sea of Marmara. 29 km. long. It has many inlets, one of which is the Golden Horn. It is of great strategic importance. Internationally controlled between 1918-36, until the Montreux Convention restored the Turkish right to fortify it.

Bursa (40 8N 29 1E) Pop. (1975) 334,941. Capital of Bursa province. Trade in tobacco, fruit, grain. Manufactures textiles, carpets. Founded in 2nd century B.C. by Prusias I of Bithynia. Captured by Ottoman Turks in 1326. Many mosques and royal Ottoman tombs.

Cappadocia (38 52N 35 30E) Mountainous area of central Turkey. In ancient times an independent kingdom, with capital at Mazaca (modern Kayseri).

Dardanelles (40 10N 26 0E) Ancient Hellespont. Strait between Asian and European Turkey, connecting Sea of Marmara to the Aegean. 72 km. (45 m.) long and 1½ to 8 km. wide. Of commercial and strategic importance. Crossed by Xerxes I in 480 B.C.; by Alexander in 334 B.C.

Eskisehir (39 20N 30 10E) Pop. (1975) 270,467. Capital of Eskişehir province. Industrial centre. Sugar refining. Manufactures textiles, cement, agricultural implements. Trade in grain. Centre of the meerschaum industry. Hot sulphur springs.

Erzurum (39 58N 41 20E) Pop. (1965) 105,300. Capital of Erzurum province. Tanning, sugar refining. Trade in grain and vegetables. Captured by Turks in 1515. Taken by Russians in 1828, 1878, 1916. Atatürk University (1957).

Gallipoli Peninsula (40 30N 26 55E) Peninsula between the Dardanelles and Gulf of Saros. Attacked by British, New Zealand, and Australian forces in 1915, and successfully defended by Turks.

Gaziantep (37 10N 37 30E) Pop. (1975) 284,564. Capital of Gaziantep province. Important market town. Manufactures textiles. Trade in grain, agricultural produce. Captured by French 1921.

Istanbul (41 1N 28 56E) Pop. (1975) 3,127,500. Capital of Istanbul province, on the Bosphorus. Turkey's chief seaport: handles most imports, many exports. Manufactures textiles, glassware, leather goods, cement. Fishing, tourism. Golden Horn harbour. Made capital of Eastern Roman empire 324 A.D. by Constantine the Great. Turkish since 1453. Capital of Turkey 1453-1923. University (1453); technical university (1773). Sixth century Byzantine Church of St. Sophia, converted to a mosque. Many 16th century mosques.

Izmir (38 21N 27 8E) Formerly Smyrna. Pop. (1975) 1,031,375. Capital of Izmir province. Seaport on the Aegean. Naval base. Exports tobacco, figs, cotton. Manufactures textiles, soap, leather goods. Early

Christian centre. Captured by Turks 1424. Greek Occupation 1919. Restored to Turkey in 1923. University (1955).

Kayseri (38 52N 35 30E) Ancient Caeserea Mazaca. Pop. (1965) 126,700. Capital of Kayseri province. Manufactures textiles, carpets, rugs, tiles. Trade in grain, fruit, vegetables. Ancient capital of Cappadocia.

Kizilirmak river (40 30N 34 15E) 1,130 km. (700 m.) long. Longest river in Asia Minor; rises in the Kizil Mountains, and flows across the Anatolian plateau to the Black Sea.

Konya (38 0N 32 35E) Ancient Iconium. Pop. (1975) 250,580. Capital of Konya province. Manufactures textiles, carpets, leather goods. Trade in wool, grain, mohair. Ancient capital of Lycaonia, visited by St. Paul. Captured by Seljuk Turks in eleventh century, and became capital.

Kurdistan (37 30N 43 30E) Region of mountain and plateau in south-east Turkey and adjacent areas of Iran, Iraq, Syria. About 2·5 million Kurds in Turkish part. Seminomads, mostly Sunni Muslims. Indo-European language.

Marmara, Sea of (40 40N 28 0E) Ancient Propontis. Named from Island of Marmara, in west. Between Asian and European Turkey. Linked by the Bosphorus to the Black Sea; by the Dardanelles to the Aegean.

Mediterranean Sea (36 0N 15 0E) Ancient Mare Internum. Connected with the Atlantic by the Strait of Gibraltar; Black Sea by Sea of Marmara, the Dardanelles, Bosphorus, and Aegean. Connected by Suez Canal to Red Sea. Almost tideless. More saline than Atlantic and Black Sea. Mild winters with moderate rain. Hot dry summers. Citrus fruit, olives, flowers on shores. Tunny and anchovy fisheries.

Sivas (39 50N 37 2E) Ancient Sebasteia. Pop. (1965) 108,300. Capital of Sivas province. Manufactures carpets, textiles. Trade in agricultural produce. Thirteenth century Seljuk buildings. National Congress in 1919.

Samsun (41 20N 36 12E) Ancient Amisus. Pop. (1965) 107,500. Capital of Samsun province, and Black Sea port. In chief tobacco region. Exports tobacco, cereals.

Tarsus (37 0N 34 50E) Ancient city, birthplace of St. Paul. Pop. (1965) 57,000. Modern market town in Eçel province. Trade in wheat, barley, fruit. Ancient ruins.

Taurus Mountains (37 30N 34 30E) Range forming southern rim of Anatolian plateau. Many peaks over 3,000 m. (10,000 ft.).

Tigris River (37 58N 40 25E) 1,850 km. (1,150 m.) long. Rises in east Turkey, flows south-east to Iraq; joins Euphrates river near Al Qurna. Flooding in late spring when Turkish snows melt. Not navigable in Turkey.

Trabzon (40 58N 39 50E) Pop. (1965) 65,500. Capital of Trabzon province, on Black Sea. Port. Exports tobacco, hazel nuts, flour. Greek colony eighth century B.C. Taken by Turks in 1461.

Van, Lake (38 30N 43 3QE) Largest salt lake in Turkey. No known outlet. Level varies from year to year. Salt and soda obtained by evaporation.

Index

TURKEY Political

Cities and Towns

International Boundaries

State Boundaries

Main Roads

Railways

Canals

Airports

Projection: Conical with two standard parallels

Scale 1:6,500,000

0   50   100   150   kilometres
0   50   100 miles

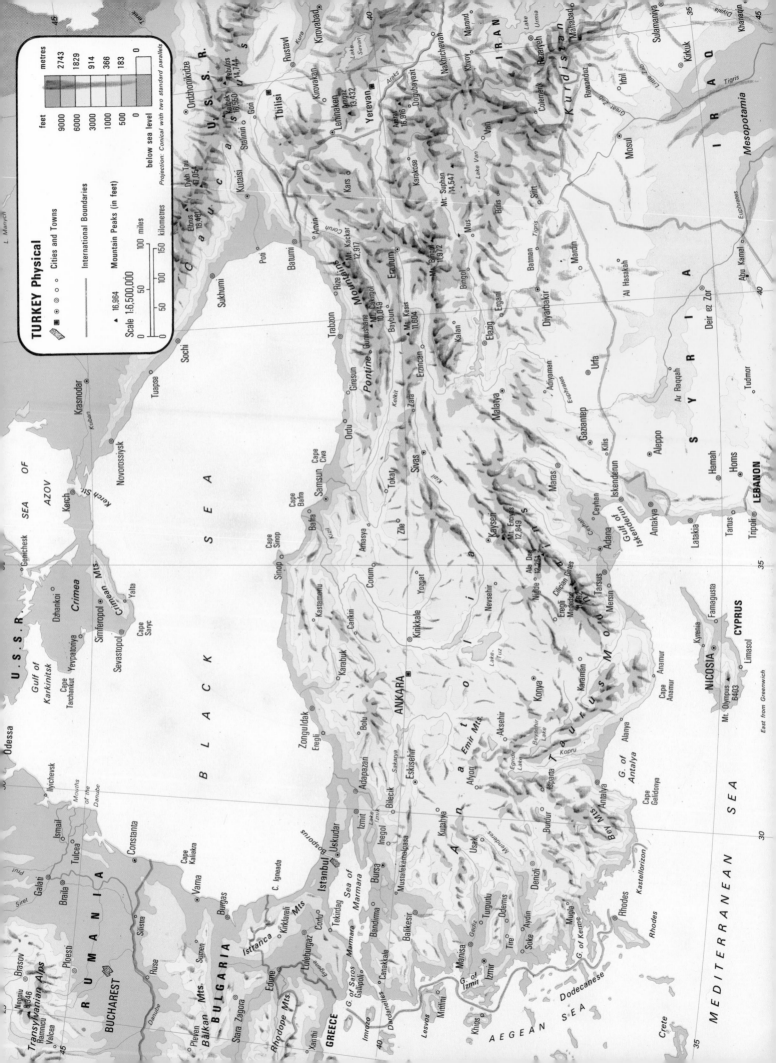